HURON COUNTY PUBLIC LIBRARY

D0024697

FEB 12

FEB 28

HURON COUNTY

F

J

51332

128.5   Walton, Douglas N
Wal   On defining death; an analytic study of
       the concept of death in philosophy and
       medical ethics. Montreal, McGill-Queen's
       University Press, 1979.
          xii, 189 p.
          Bibliography: p. 167-186.

       1. Death. 2. Euthanasia. I. Title.
       0773503315   0789631

6/61

In this book, Douglas Walton examines the philosophical nature
of two issues currently associated with medical ethics. In order to
work towards an analysis of the concept of death that could function
as a target towards which the medical criteria of death could be
directed, he proposes the foundations for a theory free of logical
contradictions, paradoxes, and other perplexities. This is the
"superlimiting theory" which introduces the notion of a "possible
person." The connection of these philosophical ideas with medico-
legal concerns like brain death and the Harvard criteria is discussed. Professor Walton then goes on to examine the difference
between killing and letting die. Through a close study of the logic
of action sentences, he develops a model that is discussed in the
light of the ethical and jurisprudential realities of medical ethics
to see if the distinction between bringing something about (actively)
and letting something happen (passively) is one that makes a
moral difference in the evaluation of actions. Numerous problematic conceptual snags are dealt with, and the author consistently
supports the conceptual clarity and respectability of the distinction.
Other relevant discriminations of an action-theoretic sort, such as
that between "direct" and "indirect" euthanasia, are studied, and
the concluding chapter applies the conceptual analysis to a philosophical discussion of attitudes towards death, asking, "Is it
rational to fear death?"

Douglas Walton teaches philosophy at the University of Winnipeg.

On Defining Death

An Analytic Study of the Concept of Death in Philosophy and Medical Ethics

Douglas N. Walton

51332

JAN 28 '80

McGILL—QUEEN'S UNIVERSITY PRESS
Montreal

© McGill-Queen's University Press 1979
International Standard Book Number 0-7735-0331-5
Legal Deposit 3rd Quarter 1979
Bibliothèque nationale du Québec
Design by Hjordis P. Wills
Printed in Canada by T. H. Best Printing Co. Ltd.

Become accustomed to the belief that death is nothing to us. For all good and evil consists in sensation, but death is deprivation of sensation. And therefore a right understanding that death is nothing to us makes the mortality of life enjoyable, not because it adds to it an infinite span of time, but because it takes away the craving for immortality. For there is nothing terrible in life for the man who has truly comprehended that there is nothing terrible in not living.

Epicurus, *Letter to Menoeceus.*

I said to the man at the gate of the Year—"Give me a light that I may tread safely into the unknown." And he replied, "Go out into the darkness and put your hand into the hand of God. That shall be to you better than light, and safer than a known way."

Christmas Broadcast of King George VI, 1939.

Contents

Acknowledgements

Research for this book was partly supported by a Canada Council leave fellowship. The first draft was written while I was on sabbatical leave from the University of Winnipeg at Victoria University of Wellington, New Zealand, in 1975–76.

Thanks are due to Professor M. J. Cresswell of Victoria University of Wellington for encouragement, assistance, and helpful discussions. Professor G. E. Hughes and Dr. J. C. Bigelow kindly read through the whole manuscript and made many valuable suggestions for improvements. My thoughts in revising were especially sharpened by discussions with Dr. Michael Tooley and Dr. John Kleinig when I read a version of chapter VII at the Australian National University and MacQuarrie University. The participants in the Philosophical Society and the Logic Seminar at Victoria University of Wellington have been responsible for many improvements, both directly and indirectly. I am especially grateful to Dr. R. L. Epstein and Dr. R. I. Goldblatt who have exerted an indirect but seminal influence on those parts related to action theory through their patient help with my struggles with the logical form of action expressions. I should mention that Dr. Peter van Inwagen stimulated many of the ideas in chapter X in a discussion we had at the Council for Philosophical Studies Conference in 1973. Dean John Woods has influenced my views considerably through his work and our discussions on the subject of death. I would like to thank Dr. Eike-Henner Kluge for reading the first draft and contributing many improvements. Professor Risto Hilpinen has made some perceptive observations and remarks concerning questions of agency in my treatment of active and passive euthanasia that resulted in some major changes and I think also some significant progress in my way of thinking about that network of categories. Dr. M. J. Newman was kind enough to read the manuscript and made many useful and illuminating remarks from the point of view of a practising neurologist. Needless to add, none of these colleagues are to be held responsible in any way for the opinions, arguments, and theories advanced in the book, or for any lapses of logic, judgement, or good taste.

I would like to thank the editors of *Ethics*, *Omega*, and *Ethics in Science and Medicine* for allowing parts of the following articles to appear in this book in various places in revised form: "Active and Passive Euthanasia," *Ethics*, 86 (1976): 269–74; "On the Rationality of Fear of Death," *Omega*, 7 (1976): 1–10; "On Logic and Methodology in the Study of Death," *Ethics in Science and Medicine*, 3 (1976): 135–47. I am indebted to the University Library of Victoria University of Wellington and the Medical School Library of the University of Auckland for assistance with obtaining materials for research. In writing the various versions of these chapters, I have been most grateful for the superb typing accuracy of Mrs. Amy Phillips, who has made my job much easier.

Preparation of the manuscript has been supported by a research grant from the University of Winnipeg. This book has been published with the help of a grant from the Humanities Research Council of Canada, using funds provided by the Canada Council.

Thanks are due to my wife for her sympathetic attitude toward my work.

Chapter I

What are the Problems?

For an appreciation of the "front line" nature of philosophical problems related to death it is necessary to see how ethical problems have arisen out of essentially practical, real-life, actual ongoing situations of medicine in the hospitals. The life-and-death-decisions of medical ethics are of course by now well known, but it is well to begin by stating them bluntly and clearly. Specifically, the two major developments of medical technology that have led directly to ethical concern about defining death are succinctly stated by Harp (1974, p. 391): "The first of these is the development of techniques for prolonged maintenance of ventilation, circulation, alimentation and excretion by artificial means, making possible the creation of a macabre situation in which the body lives while the brain is dead." The second is the widespread use of procedures of organ transplantation—in many cases, donors are patients having brain death without cessation of heartbeat. The improvement in resuscitatory procedures has led in recent years to an increasing number of patients accumulating in the hospitals who can be kept alive only by extraordinary means, for whom there is no hope of recovery. Not only are these problems so widespread that they affect each of us directly and individually, but they are so very practical that they must be thought of in a financial light. Beecher (1970, p. 472) notes: "I do not think it is crass to speak of money here, because if we had more money, we could save more lives in hospitals." But of course they are also ethical problems. The factual situations lead to and are super-imposed by ethical dilemmas. Fundamental questions of fairness and rights are at stake. The fact of organ transplantation leads to the two central moral questions of (i) when death may be said to occur, and (ii) when organ removal is permissible. These moral questions, in turn, ultimately lead to abstract philosophical questions of a semantical, purely conceptual nature, pertaining to the meaning and analysis of the terms "death" and "allow to die."[1] Although philosophy has often been criticized for being too abstract and ethereal, perhaps rightly, I think that many would now concede that there are very general philosophical questions of an abstract character directly and centrally involved in the dilemmas of death and dying, and that no treatment of these well-known ethical problems could possibly be adequate without bringing in and dealing with questions of general principles traditionally associated with the "philosophical." For one thing, it is becoming very obvious that there is much semantical confusion of a kind that could hardly be anything but "philosophical" concerning the so-called definitions of death. So if we are to get genuinely useful results, our initial problem is to recognize that we are dealing with an interdisciplinary continuum of problems, running from the concrete and practical all the way to the most abstract and theoretical, and to try to orient ourselves in order to avoid floundering around without guidance at one end or the other. We want to bring theory and practice together. That is what is needed, or at least one thing that is needed, and very badly at that. This difficulty of meshing theory and practice is, however, characteristic of recent work in medical ethics, as indicated for example by Gorovitz et al. (1976, Foreword), a standard text in the subject.

Philosophical questions arise at various junctures along the continuum. The question of whether death is equivalent to irreversible cessation of brain function is "philosophical," but obviously has practical implications as well. Juul-Jensen (1970, p. 9) points out that both practical and ethical problems are involved in the consequences of the technology that makes it possible to maintain cardiorespiratory function for long periods in patients with irreversible brain damage, since this gives rise to great financial burdens that tax the medical and nursing staffs heavily and is also often unbearable for the relatives, the only hope being that some complication will end the condition. Beecher (1970, p. 472) reports the case of a woman who was irreversibly unconscious in a Montreal hospital

1. This study is concerned with "logical foundations" in that it primarily treats of these underlying logic-semantical questions, although much of our concern lies with the applicability of logical categories to ethical dilemmas of actual medical practice.

for twelve years. Assuming that she occupied hospital space that could have been occupied by twenty-six others in a year's time, Beecher calculates that three hundred and twelve patients were kept out of a hospital bed. So perhaps it is not too hard to see how in this area ethical decisions of a practical, quality-of-life type can be connected intimately with abstract moral and semantical questions.

A primary initial problem not to be underestimated is that of sorting out the philosophical issues from the more purely medical, legal, psychological, or other specialized technical problems, and then to phrase the philosophical questions in a sufficiently precise manner to make answering possible. I do not want to put the reader off with preliminaries, but unless we precisely clarify the questions at the outset, confusion is bound to set in. Indeed, it is regrettable that at this stage of the research in medical ethics of death and dying some interdisciplinary misdirection in the formulation of objectives would seem to be evident, as we will see below. Some very real difficulties for physicians are caused in particular by confusion of two questions, in the context of death. Since each of these questions will occupy a major segment of the treatise that follows, it is well to separate them clearly at the very beginning.

Two Related but Distinct Questions

We need to make a clear distinction between the time at which a person may be rightly said to be dead and the time at which a person may be rightly allowed to die. Given a particular instance of a terminally-ill patient on a ventilator, the two "right times" may be, in effect, *the same time*, namely that time at which the ventilator is turned off by the physician in charge. Hence in practice, it is easy to conflate and confuse the question "When to allow to die?" with the question "When to declare dead?" Nevertheless, these questions are clearly different. Capron and Kass (1972, p. 105) insist rightly that the two problems must be kept separate if they are to be clearly understood: "The problem of determining when a person is dead is difficult enough without its being tied to the problem of whether physicians, or anyone else, may hasten the death of a terminally-ill patient, with or without his consent or that of his relatives, in order

to minimize his suffering or to conserve scarce medical resources."
Confusing the two questions clouds the analysis of both. We deal
with the question of the analysis of the concept of death in chapters
IV and V, and then turn to the question of the analysis of the
expression "allow to die" in subsequent chapters, where an attempt
is made to distinguish between the concepts of active and passive
euthanasia.

The question of determining death and ethical questions associated
with the notion of euthanasia intersect in many cases in practice.
For instance, consider the case of a patient with brain death[2]
whose circulating-respiratory functions are supported by artificial
ventilation. In seeking justification for shutting off the respirator,
two independent lines of argument have suggested themselves: (1)
Since the patient has *brain death*, he may be considered "dead"
(i.e., the extraordinary conditions—ventilation—require waiving the
classical circulatory-respiratory criteria of death and adopting a
brain-oriented criterion), and consequently the respirator may be
shut off. (2) The patient is alive, but shutting off the respirator is not
to *kill* him, at least actively, but is rather a mere *withdrawal of
treatment*, an "allowing of nature to take its course," an instance of
so-called passive euthanasia. We will see that it is important to
recognize that (1) and (2) are closely connected in practice, and are
not therefore, as they might initially seem, completely independent
problems. Nevertheless it is morally imperative to make a clear
distinction in thought between the two questions.

2. "Brain death" is usually characterized as total cessation of all cerebral
function—see Van Till (1975) and Juul-Jensen (1970). A detailed account of
brain death is given by Walker (1974, pp. 190f.). According to Walker, the
pathogenesis of a dead brain in a living body is "an interruption of cerebral
blood flow of sufficient duration to cause anoxic death of the high metabolizing
cerebral neurons with subsequent restoration of the circulation before other
organs of the body are destroyed." Failure of cerebral blood flow may be due to
high intercranial pressure so that blood cannot be forced into the brain, or to
heart arrest that produces the same interruption of circulation and consequent
anoxia. As a result of this anoxic process, five basic disturbances occur: (1)
failure of the blood-brain barrier; (2) breakdown of neuronal membranes; (3)
utilization of oxygen below the level required for basic metabolism of nerve
cells; (4) production and utilization of abnormal metabolic substances by the
cells (cannibalism); (5) decrease or arrest of cerebral blood flow. Thus to
establish brain death, the neurologist must use various technical procedures
(some of which are described in chapter III) to show that these basic disturbances are present.

Problems of Definition

The intertwining of the ethical problem of letting-die with that of defining death, and the connection of both with the technology of artificial ventilation is concisely expressed in a *Lancet* editorial (1974, p. 342):

> The doctor's dilemma about brain death arises only when patients are put on ventilators, and it is therefore of his own making. When a patient who already has severe brain damage develops respiratory insufficiency or cardiorespiratory arrest, careful thought should be taken before artificial respiration is extended beyond the immediate resuscitation period. Prolongation of such a patient's life, even for 12 hours (it may often be much longer in practice), reflects no credit on his doctors, particularly if this is done only so as to postpone the decision to let events take their natural course. It would be unfortunate if the time came when no patient in hospital could decently die without the last rite of modern medicine—a statutory period on the ventilator.

The two ethical problems arise from the same set of medical and social conditions, but it is necessary to be clear that the diagnosis of death must be kept separate from an interest in transplantation. A declaration of death must not be "speeded up" in a case where the patient is a potential organ donor. Beecher (1970, p. 472) rightly emphasizes this point: "Once the diagnosis of irreversible coma has been made, then and only then should the transplant team enter the picture." Clearly it is not acceptable that there should be one set of criteria for transplant donors, and another, perhaps stricter, set of criteria for those who are the potential donors.

It is obvious enough that an interest toward facilitation of transplantation could lead to a favoring of brain death as a philosophical paradigm of death. Harp (1974, p. 393) notes that while many physicians "initially were reluctant to consider organ harvest from a patient with cerebral death prior to cessation of heartbeat," the general trend in recent years has been towards acceptance of this procedure, and some transplant groups have even "abandoned attempted organ harvest *after* terminal circulatory arrest." The International Society of Transplantation (Merrill, 1971, p. 78) has stated: "We recognize that the definition of death of an individual is that of brain death rather than cardiac death." But the equation of death *simpliciter* with brain death is a hypothesis that needs to be examined at the philosophical level. Until we have a conceptual analysis of death, we are in no position to offer a philosophically adequate justification of the hypothesis that brain death is in some way equivalent to the meaning of death. The ethical question presupposes a semantical (some would say metaphysical) question. Until we have an account of *what death is*, these related questions remain mere speculation. A source of disquiet is that there seems to be a traditional, univocal conception of death according to which we seem to want to say that a person must be either unambiguously dead or not, but this traditional notion remains at an intuitive level, felt but not clearly articulated.

There are various "legal definitions" of death, but we can well ask, at a philosophical level, whether these definitions are adequate, correct, or justifiable. The legal definition of death that has evolved over the years through judicial process is given in Black's Law Dictionary, cited by Harp (1974, p. 391): "Death is the cessation of life; the ceasing to exist; defined by physicians as a total stoppage of the circulation of the blood and a cessation of the animal and vital functions consequent thereon, such as respiration, pulsation, etc." Many physicians now question the adequacy of this "definition" and alternatives are being proposed. But do these alternatives or others represent *death*, any more than the legal conceptions? Who is to say? How can it be proved? So far, these seem to be open questions, and bothersome ones at that.

The Kansas Statute

The Kansas Statute (KSA 77-202) of 1970—Capron and Kass (1972, pp. 108f.) or Taylor (1971, p. 296) may be referred to for a fuller statement—is an attempt to alleviate problems of transplantation and medical support of dying patients through legislation by offering a two-part "definition" of death. Death is "defined" first as absence of spontaneous respiratory and cardiac function, and second, as absence of spontaneous brain function:

A person will be considered medically and legally dead if, in the opinion of a physician, based on ordinary standards of medical practice, there is the absence of spontaneous respiratory and cardiac function, and, because of the disease or condition which caused, directly or indirectly, these functions to cease, or because of the passage of time since these functions ceased, attempts at resuscitation are considered hopeless; and, in this event, death will have occurred at the time these functions ceased; or

A person will be considered medically and legally dead if, in the opinion of a physician, based on ordinary standards of medical practice, there is the absence of spontaneous brain function; and if based on ordinary standards of medical practice, during reasonable attempts to either maintain or restore spontaneous circulatory or respiratory function in the absence of aforesaid brain function, it appears that further attempts at resuscitation or supportive maintenance will not succeed, death will have occurred at the time when these conditions first coincide. Death is to be pronounced before artificial means of supporting respiratory and circulatory function are terminated and before any vital organ is removed for purposes of transplantation.

These alternative definitions of death are to be utilized for all purposes in this state, including the trials of civil and criminal cases, any laws to the contrary notwithstanding.

It is not clear yet to what extent legislative attempts of this type will be successful. One difficulty with the Kansas Statute in particular is that, in boldly proposing a "definition" in two parts, it supports what is arguably a misconception, namely that there are two separate phenomena of death. See Capron and Kass (1972, p. 109) for an account of the history and background of this objection. Such a dualistic view is a particular source of public disquiet according to Kennedy (1971) insofar as it seems to sanction the inference that patient X, at a certain stage in the process of dying, may be pronounced dead, whereas patient Y, at the same stage, is not dead. The suspicion lurking behind what seems to be a too-easy pluralism is that death might be pronounced more speedily if organs are needed for transplantation. Two vexing questions in particular are thereby raised: What exactly is a "definition" in this context? That the word often appears within quotation marks suggests that it is being used in some special or even questionable way. Second, how could it be possible to have a multiple definition? How could we justify any view that entails consequences like the bizarre claim that an individual may die twice?

Given this background, the conceptual background of special categories of death like *brain death* is replete with difficulties. Juul-Jensen (1970, p. 52) writes that organ transplantations have come to stay, and that therefore "[a] clear definition of brain death, possibly laid down by the law, is a necessity." The definition of the concept of brain death, he adds, is required to facilitate the work of transplantation centers, and to assure the public "that no organ transplants will be performed unless the clinical, ethical, and human requirements are satisfied." But the philosophically troublesome question remains: what is the relation of *brain death* to *death simpliciter*? Simply because some physicians feel that brain death is an especially important or central idea of death, this in itself hardly constitutes adequate justification for the straightforward equation of death with brain death. Why is brain death thought to be especially central? Is it that the brain is regarded as the seat of consciousness in a sentient being? Why should the irreversible extinction of sensation or consciousness be so forceful as a main philosophical criterion for the death of an individual? These unanswered questions must remain a primary source of concern.

Ethical Problems of Diagnosis

Various ethical problems connected with the diagnosis of death are clearly and pointedly set out by Van Till (1975). The first reason for an especially marked need for a precise, conclusively argued diagnosis of death is the increase in causes of "apparent death."

> These include poisoning by industrial or pharmacological agents, hypothermia from a number of situations (even from winter sports or swimming), anaesthesiological, domestic or industrial accidents, and electrocution and irreversible brain stem contusions. The second reason is the possibility of organ removal. This is a real threat to the apparently dead if it is performed, as it sometimes is, without interrupting the artificial

> respiration for longer than is needed for brain neuronal death to occur, and without anaesthesia. (Van Till, 1975, p. 138)

Normally the brain dies a few minutes after cessation of heartbeat through lack of oxygen, but certain parts of the brain other than the cerebral cortex, such as that part which controls respiration, can be restored after as long as thirty minutes of oxygen deprivation. More details are given by Skegg (1974, p. 130) and for an even fuller account, the reader might look to the work of Negovskii (1962, pp. 115–17). But if resuscitation is continued after "heart death," this period of a few minutes before brain death "can be prolonged into hours or months, a period which cannot be ignored and during which much may happen" (Van Till, 1975, p. 140). Now a declaration of death means that the comatose patient is legally without rights as an existent individual from the time of the pronouncement, and therefore a too-early declaration could lead to organ removal or other "surgical assaults" on the body of a person for whom the possibility of consciousness in some form is not ruled out: "The idea that White's experiments on the perfused monkey head could be repeated in man through a premature declaration of death is utterly frightening and repugnant" (Van Till, 1975, p. 140). She refers to the 1971 experiments of White et al. Thus there are ethical problems concerning the diagnosis or determination of death as well as more abstract questions of the "definition" of death. We feel that physicians should be able to diagnose death objectively and conclusively so that there is no danger of a person who may be "alive" being treated as a corpse, an object without rights or sentient feelings. It would be in dubious taste to dwell on the horror of this sort of problem, but it is undoubtedly a major source of public disquiet and concern, and must, in the opinion of this author, be squarely faced. Even if we know what death is, how do we know, in a given case, whether it has definitely, irrevocably, and unambiguously occurred with a reasonable degree of certainty?

Of course there are numerous ethical problems of medical practice in the area of death that we will have to bypass. One fundamental issue underlying these problems that lies close to the center of the question of brain death is "What is a *person*?" When does something count as a person and when does it no longer count as being a person. This question is dealt with particularly effectively by Kluge (1975) and Tooley (1976) and readers are referred to these two treatments.

We will not deal explicitly with the question. Some of our remarks in chapter V could obviously be extended in this direction, however, by treating, in light of these remarks, the issue of whether "dead persons" exist. I will not try to pursue questions of "personhood" however, but would like to suggest this area as an open, and possibly very fruitful, line of further inquiry.

To Kill or Let Die

It is something of a scandal of medical ethics that while some distinction like that between active and passive euthanasia is widely operative in the practice of medical decision making, and even explicitly advocated in a well-known statement of the American Medical Association quoted by Rachels (1975, p. 78), the feeling of some commentators that the basis of the distinction is obscure, elusive, or even trivial[3] seems to be widely accepted and has never been rebutted. Fletcher suggests that negative euthanasia is already a fait accompli in modern medicine: "Every day in a hundred hospitals across the land decisions are made clinically that the line has been crossed from prolonging genuinely human life to only prolonging subhuman dying, and when that judgement is made respirators are turned off, life-perpetuating intravenous infusions stopped, proposed surgery cancelled, and drugs countermanded" (Fletcher, 1973a, p. 113). The problem has been forced into prominence by the development of resuscitation technology, and especially techniques for artificial ventilation, that allows physicians to prolong life even when such a course seems a pointless, painful, undignified, expensive, and hopeless postponement of imminent death. There seems to be widespread agreement that quality-of-life guidelines in the employment of these techniques are badly needed to allow us to moderate the use of "heroic and extraordinary measures" to prolong life. We already noted the *Lancet* editorial (1974, p. 342) stressing that it would be unfortunate if the time came when no patient in hospital could decently die without a statutory period on the ventilator. Thus it is often said that withdrawal of treatment under "extraordinary circumstances" from a patient who will consequently die somewhat earlier than he otherwise would, should be allowed

3. See Morison (1971), Rachels (1975), Freeman (1972), and Habgood (1974).

under certain conditions even if "active" or "positive" intervention (e.g., giving a fatal injection) is intolerable in any circumstances. The distinction is that between (active) killing and (passive) letting-die. Of course the word "euthanasia" is such that its emotive connotations tend to warp its import from one person to another, but for those to whom this word is not entirely objectionable, the distinction in question may be posed as that between active and passive euthanasia.

To one who thinks in terms either of the intentions of the agent or the consequences of the action, there seems to be no real ethical difference at all between active and passive euthanasia, and as Morison (1973) notes, such a distinction seems to many "irrelevant logic-chopping." A situational ethicist, for example, might prefer to focus on the scene itself and the demands of concrete circumstances rather than be carried away by the apparent red herring of such abstractions. Morison himself (1973, p. 60) points out, however, that even though "there may be a trivial intellectual distinction between active and passive euthanasia," the overwhelming majority recoil from active measures, such as injecting poison or an air bubble into a vein, and this factor, coupled with the widespread acceptance of passive measures, forces one to a recognition of the practical importance of the distinction. According to Morison, defending positive euthanasia would simply be futile, in the face of the reluctance of a vast majority to accept it at the present time. Thus if there is a basis for the distinction, it is a matter of some practical importance to try to find out where it lies.

Yet another medical problem forces the need to explore this issue. While some years ago few physicians were enthusiastic about treating children with meningomyeloceles, more recently there has been increasing interest in early, vigorous, and comprehensive treatment. Freeman (1972, p. 905) notes, however, that one of the leading exponents of such treatment has recently stated that not all children with meningomyeloceles should be treated: "We are thus between the Scylla of treating all children with meningomyeloceles with resultant increase in the number of survivors with severe handicapping conditions, and the Charybdis of not treating some children and permitting nature to take its often long, lingering course." Freeman (1972, p. 905) argues that since, in deciding to treat or not to treat, the physician is making a decision between life or death (for or against passive euthanasia or "letting nature take its course"), why should the physician not "also have the opportunity to alleviate the pain and suffering by accelerating that death?" Would it not be more humane to end the pain and suffering rather than to allow the child with unoperated meningomyeloceles to lie around a ward for weeks, or months, waiting to die in painful death?[4] What is the basis for accepting passive euthanasia but condemning active intervention if the latter appears the more humane alternative? Morally, is there any sound basis for advocating one but not the other? Is there really any significant difference here at all?

The natural response resides in the suggestion that in the case of active euthanasia there is a positive action involved, an overt episode of conduct or behavior on the part of the physician, whereas in the passive case this element is lacking. One can "let something happen" without (so to speak) doing anything at all. In flat rebuttal to this apparently innocent and straightforward way of drawing the distinction is the fact that turning off a ventilator, an act thought in the usual kind of case under discussion to constitute passive euthanasia, is an actual, overt episode of conduct. Thus certain instances of letting-happen apparently do require some form of positive, overt behavior. What seems the natural basis of the distinction is simply untenable, and we are left in a state of *aporia*. Perhaps the distinction is merely sophistical or trivial at bottom, we seem forced to admit. We are challenged to find an alternative basis for it, for if there is no genuine, workable, rational difference after all, then all those supporters of passive euthanasia can hardly defend their rejection of active euthanasia with any basis in logic. We attempt to meet this challenge in chapters VII and VIII, through the analysis of the concept of human action.

The question here is whether there is an analysis of the concept of human action in contexts of moral responsibility that allows us to clearly explicate the distinction between "making-happen" and "letting-happen" in a way that throws some light on the often cited but inchoate and intuitive distinction between active and passive euthanasia. If there is such a distinction, is it more than mere "logic-chopping"—is it the morally appropriate distinction to make? Does it imply that "letting-happen" is always permissible, or if it implies that "letting-happen" is weaker, or less serious than "making-happen," how can this implication be shown to have a defensible logical structure?

4. Compare the remark of Rachels (1975) on Down's syndrome.

Thanatophobia

To complement empirical psychological studies that quite properly comprise the bulk of the scientific literature on fear and anxiety about death, it is helpful to investigate the underlying logic of death-related concepts by philosophical and semantical methods.[5] Accordingly, here we will adopt a frankly decision-theoretic approach according to which the behavior of actual decision makers may or may not conform to the principles under discussion. In other words, we will not be concerned directly with the question of how fear of death is exhibited behaviorally, but with the quite distinct although not unrelated question of the conditions under which it might be said to be rational for a person to fear death.[6] I do not wish to assert, of course, that we are, or even should be or can be, "rational" about death, but only that it is interesting to investigate some semantical and logical conditions under which one might consistently be said to be "rational" about death.

According to the widely prevalent *secular conception of death*, death is to be thought of as irreversible, and total extinction of consciousness and sensation, including discontinuation of actual survival of the individual personality.[7] The broadly *religious conception of death* postulates, by contrast, some form of actual survival of the individual personality and accompanying continuation of *post mortem* consciousness and sensation. We shall be concerned here primarily with certain logical consequences of the secular conception that do not appear to be widely consistently understood or clearly appreciated. This concern is not to be interpreted as an endorsement of, or

5. See also Kastenbaum and Aisenberg (1972).

6. We will require in general that a "rational" person be logically consistent. Beyond that it is difficult to explicate this key term adequately much further at this point except to disavow any psychiatric implications. It suffices for our admittedly restricted purposes in this chapter to understand "rational" generally in a decision-theoretic sense, although the work undertaken here is really preliminary to understanding the fuller meaning of rationality in relation to thanatophobia. But see also Krieger and Epting (1974), Lester (1967), and Feifel and Branscomb (1973). Professor E.-H. Kluge has pointed out to me that a narrow definition of "rational" in terms of logical consistency does not seem to be fully adequate. I may be irrational for periods and still be a rational being. I may also be inconsistent unbeknownst to me or anyone else and therefore be "irrational" in the sense of being logically inconsistent, but not be irrational according to anyone's knowledge here and now.

7. See the discussion and background given by Choron (1963).

argument for, one conception over the other. Since both are widely held, both views need to be studied.[8] A significant problem is, however, that there are seminal inconsistencies and paradoxes in the secular conception. The full logical import of this view has, for whatever reasons, not been traditionally drawn out in any very serious, protracted, consistent philosophical or theoretical treatment.[9] Thus, for example, it may not seem apparent how it could be rational to fear death at all if death is accompanied by irreversible absence of sensation or consciousness. The ancient Stoic and Epicurean controversies come to mind: it seems irrational to fear *nothing*, the utter lack of individual existence.[10] Heuristically then, we approach the question this way: on the secular conception, what is it about death that could be consistently said to constitute a proper object of fear or anxiety?

In order to approach this seminal question, we will examine one of its important underlying presuppositions, namely the anterior question of whether and how death can be assigned a negative value. We will focus specifically on the more restricted question of the conditions under which death might be said to constitute an evil, a tragic event, or a negative outcome generally, whatever standard of value might be applied. On a strict secular hypothesis, it is not immediately evident that death can reasonably be said to constitute an event that can be assigned a negative value. To turn to this question, we outline two varieties of the secular conception of death in chapter V, and proceed from there to examine the question of whether it is rational to fear death, on the secular hypothesis, in chapter XI.

A New Approach

Increasing acquaintance with the recent literature on bio-medical, legal, and psychological aspects of death tends to have a progressive effect of eroding our traditional ideas about death to the point where

8. But see the interesting discussion of Kübler-Ross (1969, pp. 14f.).

9. Reasons for this are given by Choron (1963).

10. Epicurus in ancient writings (translated here in a version published in 1964) characterized death as deprivation of sensation. "Death is nothing to us; for what has been dissolved has no sensation, and what has no sensation is nothing to us" (*Principal Doctrines*, II).

one may well begin to question whether there is any single clear, consistent notion of the basic concept of death that underlies our varied concerns. We may conclude: let technology take us where it will, and let us not prejudice the issues by making abstract or philosophical demands—an integrated physiological system does not fail at one uniquely identifiable moment according to Morison (1971). This study, on the contrary, will act on the assumption that we cannot pull ourselves up by our bootstraps, that in redefining or defining *death* we are defining something that is familiar to us and describable if in an essentially loose sort of way, that in giving criteria for death (see chapter III) we offer criteria for something that is partially understood in advance. To give shape to this "something" we set out in chapters IV and V a conceptual analysis of death in two stages: (i) a set of adequacy conditions for any analysis of a standard notion of death, and (ii) a specific analysis of death that meets this set of conditions. The purpose of the analysis is to assist bio-medical, legal, ethical, and psychological inquiry by explicating a central and important concept of death that underlies our multidisciplinary concerns, yet has not been fully articulated in a philosophically adequate or conceptually clear way.

It is important to understand some limitations of the project of constructing a conceptual analysis of death. This project is no substitute for, nor does it provide automatic answers to, operational questions of medical technology concerning criteria for the determination of the occurrence of death. But it will help us better to understand the conceptual basis of these criteria by explaining and clarifying what it is that these criteria are supposed to determine. Nor will this analysis yield *automatic* answers to ethical questions of euthanasia, or psychological questions of thanatophobia, but by clarifying the concept of death it will assist us to phrase these questions with greater clarity and objectivity, and less conceptual confusion, and thereby provide general guidelines. Thus our analysis is best seen as a foundational adjunct to, not as a replacement for, empirical, ethical, and technological inquiries. It would certainly be an error to encourage empty philosophical theorizing at the expense of our very real practical and empirical concerns. Yet to coordinate practical inquiries, some degree of theoretical abstraction is at this stage very useful. What is needed is a logic of death, or "methodologic," to borrow a word from Kastenbaum and Aisenberg (1972).

Chapter II

Levels of Defining Death

Concepts and Criteria

At the outset it is necessary to appreciate clearly the need for a broad distinction between the analysis of the meaning of a concept and the essentially epistemic question of how that concept is known to be instantiated in a particular case. In order to dispel some of the grosser semantical confusions, it is essential to distinguish between analyzing the meaning[1] of death and establishing operational criteria for death. Admittedly, it is hard to know how much weight this informal yet very general distinction will bear if it is examined thoroughly at a high level of metaphysical or epistemological inquiry. But the literature on death we will examine cries out for some such basic form of distinction as an initial prerequisite, and I see no alternative to making it, or at least allowing it, even if such terms as *meaning* and *epistemic* may be ultimately problematic. Kass (1971, p. 699) distinguishes between the meaning of an abstract concept and the operations used to determine or measure it, suggesting that the phrase "definition of death" should be used only with respect to the first, and "criteria for determining that a death has occurred" for the second. Certainly the two projects are connected, even intimately, but failure to recognize that at least two relatively

---

1. We will not attempt to say in general what the meaning of a concept consists in, but the process of explication of the concept of death in chapters IV and V may be regarded as an attempt at explication in the sense of Carnap (1950, Introduction). According to Carnap, a concept is successfully explicated where it meets a set of well-defined conditions indicating a match or resemblance to the notion it explicates, and as well, the explication is relatively clear, consistent, and fruitful in leading to new knowledge. Also, other things being equal, a simpler explication is preferable. Similar methodology is applicable to the explication of action given in chapters VII, VIII, and IX.

distinct basic levels of inquiry are involved, each requiring to some extent its own framework of methodology and expertise, is a heuristic obstacle blocking the most elementary form of inquiry into the foundations of the medical ethics of death. The phrases "definition of death" and "redefinition of death" are deeply ambiguous, and often appear highly misleading in this respect. In particular, they may seem to indicate that the development of new proposed criteria automatically, on a one-to-one basis, necessitate radical changes in the meaning of the traditional concept of death, and that physicians should be able straightforwardly to dictate such changes through new diagnostic procedures, or to pronounce simply on the basis of diagnostic developments of a technical sort that there is more than one "death." This is quite properly thought to be absurd, paradoxical, or even outrageous.[2] We may presume that by "definition," at least in the wider social and ethical context, more is involved than merely bare criteria in the sense of technical medical methods for the determination of death in a given case.

The problem is that the very terms "defining death" and "definition of death" are conducive to misunderstanding and confusion. Concerning these terms Capron and Kass (1972, p. 88) write: "Though it would be desirable not to use such terms, they are too well established in professional and public discourse on these matters to be eliminated." However, if we are to stick with these terms, as seems inevitable anyway, it is worthwhile stressing that at least two levels of "definition" must be involved. Cassell, Kass, et al. (1972, p. 49) follow many others in distinguishing between "controversy concerning proper procedures for determining death" and "controversy concerning the proper concept of death." They also wisely caution (p. 51) that it is best to avoid the notion that the new criteria of death "constitute a new or an alternative *definition* of death, rather than a refined and alternative means for detecting the same 'old' phenomenon of death." We may fairly safely presume that the question of *criteria* is virtually exclusively a technical medical issue, whereas in regard to the question of the *concept* of death such a presumption would be highly unsafe, or at least open to widespread disagreement. The concept of death is not only multidisciplinary but also heavily philosophical in content.

2. See Kennedy (1971).

Conceptual Analysis

Capron and Kass (1972, p. 94) agree that the idea of death is at least partly a philosophical question and not "simply a technical matter nor one susceptible of empirical verification." But they note that the underlying extra-medical aspects of the question only become visible when medicine begins to depart from the common or traditional understanding of death. Thus they distinguish aspects of formulating a "definition" of death over and above the "criteria" or "tests" of death that surely do come within the sphere of purely medical expertise. All this suggests that it is reasonable to require that an understanding of death that would be genuinely helpful in dealing with problems of medical ethics would have to meet the dual requirement of being (a) philosophically adequate in the sense of being capable of being brought into relation to the layman's concept of the traditional notion of death, and (b) medically adequate in relation to those very developments in medical technology that have created the need to deal with these problems in the first place. Hence a useful philosophical analysis of death must be formulated at the abstract, theoretical level, but anchored in the practicalities of medicine's daily life-and death working decisions.

Even if it is agreed that we at least intuitively or partially understand the notion of death as laymen, why should any further philosophic refinement of the notion be necessary or desirable? The answer is that the phenomenon of death must function as a goal for diagnosis. Van Till (1975, p. 139) argues in this spirit that a philosophical conception of death is a necessary adjunct to an adequate method of diagnosis of death: "a definition of death is indispensable in order to compile a diagnosis of death. Otherwise the target at which the diagnosis 'aims at' is unknown." To be sure, it is not too difficult to see that there is a conceptual side to death and that it requires some form of philosophical analysis to best understand it. Even the most recalcitrant pragmatist or skeptic might go along with us this far. A more difficult skepticism to cope with might be based on the pluralism of our notions of death. Obviously death is an important legal problem as Capron and Kass (1972) and Skegg (1974) indicate, and not less a problem for social and behavioral scientists. Moreover, concepts like "brain death" seem to occupy an intermediate position in our two levels. These complications suggest a multi-level approach to the question of definition. Purely philosophical analysis must be involved at the higher levels, to provide a "target" for diagnosis, but various other levels of empirical inquiry need to be interposed between the purely conceptual level and the operational base level of diagnosis.

A Multi-Levelled Approach

Various authors have suggested a more fine-grained approach to the question of definition. Cassell, Kass, et al. (1972, p. 52) distinguish *five* levels at which decisions are made with respect to the death of a human being: (1) establishing a concept of death; (2) selecting general criteria and procedures for determining that a patient has died; (3) determining in the particular case that the patient meets the criteria; (4) pronouncing him dead; (5) certifying the death on a certificate of record. Once having appreciated the distinction between general criteria and the more specialized activities of (3), (4), and (5), we can see with greater clarity that there need be no conflict between the specialized role of the physician and the process of abstract inquiry into the concept of death. The latter is one aspect of level (1) that bears on level (2) but only more obliquely on the remaining three levels.

Yet another very useful multi-levelled sketch interposes a new level (2), between theory (1) and criteria (3) and (4). According to the approach of Capron and Kass (1972, pp. 102ff.) there are at least four levels of "definition" of the notion of death as a transition from the state of being alive to the state of being dead. (1) The *basic concept* of death is a philosophical matter of abstract definitions that influences the devising of standards and criteria for death, but offers little concrete help in the practical question of determining whether an individual has died. (2) The level of *general physiological standards* is more medico-technical, but still partly philosophical, since we must choose in what terms death is to be defined, for example, organ systems, physiological functions, or human capacities. Capron and Kass offer the following examples of possible general standards: "irreversible cessation of spontaneous respiratory and/or circulatory functions," "irreversible loss of spontaneous brain functions," "irreversible loss of the ability to communicate." (3) *Operational criteria* further define what is meant in (2). For example, "cessation of spontaneous circulatory functions" might be specified by the criteria of lack of cardiac contraction or blood circulation. (4) *Specific tests and procedures* indicate whether the criteria are met, EEG measurements, pulse, blood pressure, and so forth.

The important concept of brain death seems partly medical (technical) and partly philosophical in make-up, and therefore occupies an intermediate position between (1) and (3). In my opinion, this important concept (along with the other well-known hybrids such as "cell death" and so forth) belongs, wherever else it may also be relevant, in the area of level (2). Brain death is often thought to be a technical notion, but at the same time it is of philosophical significance in medical ethics. Studies of medical-diagnostic criteria are sometimes oriented specifically to what seems to be a purely technical, physiological notion of brain death. Here we might cite the studies of Jørgenson, Jørgenson and Rosenklint (1973), Juul-Jensen (1970), Ingvar et al. (1974), Robinson (1972), and Mohandas and Chou (1971). For example *brain death* is defined in the first study as "irreversible cessation of all brain function." But there are many areas also of philosophical concern. Is brain death merely one type of death (opposed, say, to respiratory death)? Is brain death simply equatable with death, or is brain death a concept that belongs on a different level than the concept of death *simpliciter?*[3] The formulation of these and related questions suggests the philosophical content of level (2) of inquiry. Once we have arrived at a level (1) hypothesis, we will still apparently find that many philosophically tinged questions at the second level remain concerning the implementation and orientation of that concept.

Recognition of these multiple levels of definition may help to dispel or at least reduce some confusions about the plurality of "definitions." The notion that there are several kinds of death, that is, alternative definitions of death, is cited in Kennedy (1971) as a source of public disquiet and misunderstanding because, of course, common sense seems to dictate that death is univocal, even if the

---

3. One might want to argue of course that there is a plurality of kinds of death. I do not find such pluralism easily acceptable. Perhaps this position can be made more acceptable by arguing that the respiratory-circulatory notion of death is appropriate in normal circumstances, whereas a brain-oriented notion is appropriate in certain extraordinary circumstances, i.e., where artificial ventilation is present. For further discussion, see Morgan and Kass (1972), Skegg (1974), and Halley and Harvey (1968).

criteria for death might vary according to differing needs or purposes. Kennedy feels, no doubt echoing a widespread sentiment, that clearly there are not two kinds of death, and the statement of the Kansas Statute that there are alternative definitions is therefore to be rejected as a misconception. He insists, not without reason, that there must be one point, however arbitrary, that is considered death (p. 948). Otherwise we are faced with the *prima facie* unacceptable consequence that one person, at a certain stage in the process of dying, can be pronounced dead, while another person, at the very same stage, is not said to be dead. Perhaps some form of irreducible pluralism concerning death might eventually arise from developments in medical diagnosis. It is certainly too early to say. But taking a multi-levelled approach at least shows us that a plurality of diagnostic techniques on the lower levels need not imply a conceptual pluralism at level (1) or (2).

Recognition of the level of general physiological standards in particular helps us to understand the apparent twilight zone between medicine and philosophy in which certain hypotheses on death are formulated. Van Till (1975, p. 137) distinguishes between the philosophical definitional level (death is "the total and permanent disintegration of the psychosomatic entity") and the level of diagnosis, but interposes a hypothesis in the form of an equation between these two levels: "This disintegration takes place if and when brain death occurs and only then." She clarifies a bit further: "Brain death is the irreversible absence of all brain function." She further posits that since comatose patients have some brain function left, irreversible (probably incurable) coma is not identical with brain death. I suggest that these hypotheses, apparently occupying an intermediate zone between (1) and the lower levels, might occur at stratum (2).

We could sum up by concluding that three important, fairly distinct areas of inquiry of significant philosophical concern each of which is one aspect of "defining death" are: the basic concept, general physiological standards, and operational criteria. The third area, and to a large degree the second, come within the scope of the authority of medical expertise. The first area is heavily philosophical. But a purely abstract philosophical analysis, if it is to be any use in medical ethics, must to a certain extent take these findings relevant at the other levels into account and comment on them. Only then can we turn to purely conceptual questions.

Skepticism

Those of a strongly relativistic bent are bound to remain feeling that any real progress at the conceptual level is impossible, and that individual cases can only be strictly defined by their particular circumstances.[4] This position of skepticism is forcefully represented by Morison (1971), who argues that the popular notion of death as an event that takes place at a discrete point of time is simply a misleading figure of speech, a personified abstraction that fallaciously introduces an artificial discontinuity into what is essentially a continuous process. Morison suggests that the illusion that there is a single unique "moment of death" is only made plausible by the fact that the tripartite system of respiration, circulation, and cerebration seems to fail, under natural conditions, at one time. Thus traditionally, observers of the climatic agony of the well-known phenomenon of a "singularly violent last gasping breath" found it easy to believe that some special event, Death, has taken place (Morison, 1971, p. 695). Given recent technological developments however, it has become known that an integrated physiological system does not all fail at once, and consequently death may be viewed more accurately as an indeterminate process of decline with no single, clear, non-arbitrary cut-off point. Morison urges that instead of toying with redefinition, we ought instead to recognize that a life may reach a state where we are not ethically obliged to preserve it, and thus a quality-of-life decision must be made that it can be terminated when the benefits decline and the costs, pain, and suffering mount correspondingly higher. Morison offers no guidelines for making such quality-of-life decisions, rather counselling circumspection and caution, founded on a position of ethical relativism and emphatic rejection of "absolute standards."[5]

Given a viewpoint of extreme ethical relativism, any objective conceptual analysis of death appears to be ruled out to begin with,[6] but even granting that quality-of-life decisions are involved, it is not obvious that an initial relativism about them need be presupposed. Ethical relativism of this extreme variety has always had

4. Note the interesting discussions of moral relativism in medical ethics in Kluge (1975, pp. 236–42).
5. But see the counter-argument of Kass (1971).
6. See the various discussions of Kluge (1975).

its exponents, but it is hardly a view of values that can be adopted uncritically, or that represents the only possible point of view. A more balanced approach is found in McCormick (1974), who also draws attention to the need for quality-of-life judgements in the face of medical technology that can keep almost anyone alive. McCormick cites the two extremes of vitalism (life at any cost) and medical pessimism that characterize aspects of the Judeo-Christian tradition —both extremes view death as an evil. McCormick then gives sensitive arguments for steering a middle course to view life as a relative good. Support of life under extraordinary conditions of grave hardship can be a disproportionate effort for sheer survival that in no way contributes to the fullness of a life, and indeed may threaten, strain, or submerge the possibilities of growth in love of God and neighbor that are often traditionally thought to constitute the central meaning of life. Life is rather the condition of other values than an overriding, absolute value in itself—"life is a value to be preserved only insofar as it contains some potentiality for human relationships" (McCormick, p. 175). Thus even given a quality-of-life point of view, it is possible to adopt an ethical approach that is not so situational as to favor an extreme skepticism about philosophical analysis and broad conceptual quidelines.

Skepticism of a similar sort may be implied in the often-expressed belief that the problem is exclusively medical. The belief that the matter of "defining death" is wholly medical is cited as widespread by Capron and Kass (1972, p. 92), and Skegg (1974, p. 132) states that it is an almost unanimous view in British legal circles that the question is simply and wholly a medical one. The report of Richardson, Rosenheim, et al. (1970, p. 750) states that there is no distinct group of clinical signs that always indicate conclusively that death has occurred. The opinion of the committee for this report is that the determination of death must be a matter of the individual doctor's judgement. Rozovsky (1972, p. 24) quotes Lord Kilbrandon as citing the problem as an exclusively medical matter: "[the question of the moment of death] is a technical, professional matter. It is entrusted to medical men to say when a man is dead, and nobody but a doctor can decide that." Of course the only final way to rebut the skeptic's charge is to present a conceptual analysis that is acceptable to him, but some remarks may suffice to show that Morison and other skeptics have not shown that it is not possible to evolve such an analysis. First, if a change is gradual or continuous, it does not follow that it cannot be located. Second, as Kass (1971, p. 699) stresses, it is the death of the individual human being that is important for physicians and the community, not the "death" of organs or cells, which are only parts of the whole organism. Kass observes that a proof that death is not a discrete event would require evidence that the organism as a whole died progressively and continuously, and this kind of evidence is nowhere given, for example, by Morison. There is a danger of fallacy in arguing from properties of the parts to a property of the whole (fallacy of composition). Third, given our appreciation of the ramified nature of the levels of definition, we should not expect the conceptual level to provide a mechanism that can quantitatively pinpoint a "moment of death" for this (or something like it) is the function of the criteria. In summary, the skeptical argument of Morison does not yield conclusive evidence that a conceptual analysis of the traditional notion of death is not possible, but does show that one does not presently exist. It therefore may serve as a challenge, but not as a rebuttal to the project itself.

Legal and Medical Definitions

There is no *prima facie* reason to believe at this point that the conceptual aberrations posed by the recent developments in medical technology require a complete "redefinition" of the traditional notion of death. For any empirical concept has a quality of open texture according to Waismann (1965) in not being sharply defined in new or unusual situations. Only an analysis of the traditional notion will yield an idea of the modifications or extensions required to cope with new cases. Skegg (1974, p. 133) suggests that while there may be a fundamental distinction between human life and death, "our conceptual unities have sharp edges non-existent in nature." Yet for legal purposes, it may be necessary to make a sharp distinction between the living and the dead. One of the blurred edges taken up by Skegg that is very much at issue is the question of whether "irreversibly comatose" individuals are alive or dead. An irreversibly comatose individual is defined by Skegg (1974, p. 130) as referring to "those persons who, although traditionally considered alive, have sustained such brain damage that there is no possibility of their returning to any form of consciousness." Conceding that whether someone is irreversibly comatose is a question of "medical fact," there remains the non-medical-technical question of whether such a person is dead. That there are significant areas of vagueness in the term "dead" is something that should worry us. But in some respects "redefinition" is too strong a word. For one thing, it suggests that we already have a definition. It might also suggest that there is hidden inconsistency in the concept of death.

But might one significant obstacle to the philosophical analysis of death be the possibility of inconsistency between medical and legal accounts of death? That is, a given person at a given state might be "medically dead" but "legally not dead."[7] How could a unified philosophical analysis at the conceptual level possibly deal with that sort of conflict? Granted, if this sort of inconsistency existed, it might make the idiom of "redefinition" appropriate. Some writers suggest that there is evidence of such inconsistencies. Halley and Harvey (1968, p. 105) argue that the "inclusive" legal definition and the "ordinary" medical definition of death, while somewhat different in language and approach, exhibit a general symmetry, adumbrated as follows.

Commonly Accepted but Unofficial (Ordinary) Medical Definition	Evolving but Unofficial Legal Definition
1. Insensibility	1. Cessation of "vital functions"
2. Cessation of respiration	2. Cessation of respiration
3. Cessation of circulation	3. Cessation of circulation
4. Irreversibility	4. Impossibility of resuscitation

In contrast, an "extraordinary" (e.g., brain-oriented) medical definition of death, they suggest, might be employed "when a person with a totally and permanently destroyed central nervous system is sustained by artificial means." Unlike the "ordinary" definition above, the "extraordinary" medical definition, Halley and Harvey add, is actually inconsistent with the legal definition. We add parenthetically here that the expression "extraordinary means" is a relative phrase—relative to the circumstances, availability of resources, and the willingness to employ them. This relativity is explicated in the treatment of Kluge (1976, p. 156). Thus to tie the notion of death to the notion of extraordinary means makes death

7. The same problem arises for various other possible interdisciplinary conflicts, and some of the remarks in the sequel may apply to these cases as well.

itself a relative matter. Consequently a too heavy reliance on this expression in attempting to define death is to be cautioned against, unless of course one wishes to take a frankly relativistic stance toward the concept of death.

Quite clearly, just as there is a ramified relationship between medical-technical data and any reasonable philosophical theory, as indicated by our account of the various levels of definition, there will be a similar phenomenon of multi-levelled relationship between legal and philosophical considerations. Relevant legal developments cannot be ignored in evaluating a conceptual analysis, and it would be hoped that the latter would be of some help in understanding the logical foundations of legal notions of death. At the outset, however, it would be premature to posit an irreducible inconsistency between medical and legal views. Cassell, Kass, et al. (1972, p. 51) suggest that the opposition between medical and legal points of view is often exaggerated by misleading language, and that the law treats the actual biological phenomenon of death as a medical question of fact, to be determined by physicians. So-called legal definitions of death, rather than standing in any opposition to medical "fact," are rather directed to other purposes such as determining inheritance or survivorship. To be sure, medical considerations have a certain primacy, both in relation to philosophical and to legal theory.

On the other hand, in order to be of value, a philosophical theory must not be a mere compendium of "medical fact," and must strive to bring constraints of theory to bear on these data. I hope we have by now made clear that we are not dealing with a wholly and exclusively medical problem. McCormick suggests that few doctors are willing to establish guidelines and "moral theologians," in a concern to avoid arbitrariness, can easily be insensitive to the moral relevance of the raw experience, with the result that the ethical alternatives are reduced to *dogmatism* (which imposes a formula that prescinds from circumstances) and *pure concretism* (which denies the possibility or usefulness of any guidelines). On the other hand, it is a fact that life-or-death ethical decisions are being made every day,[8]

---

8. Dr. M. J. Newman has made some valuable remarks from the point of view of a practising neurologist that may serve to put our inquiry in a more mature perspective. Looking at the question of saving life from a practical point of view, death cannot be prevented, but only postponed. Doctors in fact do not make as many decisions of life or death as the ethical discussions might lead us to believe. Often it might seem so, "but in many cases, the disease is

and therefore we can hardly abstain from taking the responsibility of analyzing these judgements to abstract from them the criteria inescapably operative in them (McCormick, 1974, p. 173). To do otherwise is to exempt these decisions from the critique and control that protects against abuse. Thus a middle course of broad guidelines or substantive standards is both possible and necessary, even though the reasons given contain intuitive elements, grounded in beliefs and profound feelings, that enter into any judgement of this kind. McCormick (p. 173) uses the analogy: a guideline is not a slide rule, but more like a light in a room that allows the individual objects in it to be seen in the fullness of their context.

So far we have not found any conclusive reason to believe that the concept of death is insusceptible to any form of objective analysis, inherently opaque, unanalyzable, or inconsistent. All we have found is that we don't know very much about it, and that it is vague in rather important, worrisome ways. In other words, it is clear enough that we don't have an analysis of it that will satisfy the skeptics or alleviate our problems, but it has not been shown that we can't analyze it. On the other hand, we have seen lots of reasons why the project will not be easy or simple. But perhaps we should not be discouraged. At least, not yet.

---

likely to progress to death regardless of what the doctor does and his intervention is only a very partial one in the course of nature." (Remark in private correspondence.) Accordingly, it is somewhat wiser to frame the question more in terms of whether medical intervention is likely to be efficacious and for the good of the patient and less in terms of "life and death."

Chapter III

Criteria for the Determination of Death

Traditional and "New" Criteria

The "new" criteria for death have evolved not to produce a replacement or successor in every instance for the traditional clinical means of diagnosis such as pulse, heartbeat, and respiration, but rather to supply an ancillary method of diagnosis in certain special cases that arise through the widespread use of new medical technology. In particular, it is the use of machines for artificial ventilation that leads to the situation where a patient may be kept "alive" (by traditional criteria, including respiration) for a prolonged period in which virtually all brain function has irreversibly ceased.[1] In cases where artificial ventilation is not used, normally all brain function ceases irreversibly within a short period of time after cessation of respiration and circulation, and consequently the need for a distinction between death generally and "brain death" simply does not arise.

In this chapter we will give a sampling of some of what seem to be the most significant developments among the various proposed sets of criteria that have been put forward. Our review is by no means complete, nor can it pretend to be entirely representative of the issues from a medical point of view. But it should give the reader a fair idea of what is involved generally, as background for an intelligent and reasonably informed consideration of the related conceptual and ethical issues.

An account of the traditional, clinical criteria for death is given by Hillman (1972, pp. 88f.). These criteria are used in "ordinary" cases by "the jobbing physician"—criteria for the transplant surgeon in "extraordinary" cases, where the patient has irreversible

---

1. Some care of statement is needed here. I am told by a transplant surgeon that prolonged maintenance of a properly brain-dead patient is not possible, because of the almost invariable destruction of the vasomotor center. Hence the qualification, "virtually."

brain damage but is artificially ventilated, are described quite differently. The "ordinary" criteria are as follows: (1) relevant medical history of the condition thought to have led to death; (2) absence of pulse and heart beat; (3) absence of respiration; (4) absence of movement or reflexes; (5) pupillary dilation; (6) glassy corneas; (7) patchy pallor and cyanosis of the skin; (8) irreversibility of signs (2)–(7). It is pointed out that the signs are reversible if due to drowning or hypothermia (and any sign may be due to various non-fatal causes), and thus irreversibility alone distinguishes death from hypothermia or drowning. Since irreversibility is a "retrospective" criterion, it imposes on the physician the responsibility to attempt resuscitation wherever possible.

The new criteria are most often set forth as criteria of "brain death," and are notably different from the traditional criteria in emphasizing means of diagnosing brain activity or brain function. The new criteria normally require absence of spontaneous breathing, but do allow that a patient in whom the respiratory function is supported artificially may be considered "brain dead."

The Harvard Criteria

The most prominent set of criteria is the "Report of the Ad Hoc Committee of the Harvard Medical School to Examine Brain Death" (Beecher, 1968), which offers essentially the following criteria: (1) unreceptivity and unresponsiveness to external stimuli; (2) no spontaneous muscular movement or spontaneous breathing; (3) no reflexes, including brain and spinal reflexes; (4) isoelectric (flat) electroencephalogram; (5) all of the above to be re-verified after twenty-four hours; (6) the patient not to be hypothermic (temperature below 32.2°C) or under the influence of central nervous system depressants. (See also the summaries in Cassell, Kass, et al., 1972, p. 49, and Harp, 1974, p. 392.) The twenty-four hour delay is explained by the fact that the Harvard criteria were designed with the question in mind of when to shut off the ventilator without consideration of the question of organ transplantation. Thus the criteria are set to deal with cases where resuscitation machinery is in use and where consequently the traditional signs of death are obscured—they are not meant to replace the traditional criteria in all circumstances, rather only in what are sometimes called "heroic" or "extraordinary" circumstances, for example by Beecher (1968a).

The electroencephalograph (EEG) is a machine that records bio-electric potentials generated by the living brain. Harp (1974, p. 393) notes that according to a 1970 report of the American Electro-encephalographic Society, only three survived out of a study of 2,642 patients reported to have isoelectric EEG readings. All three were drug overdose cases.

There have been criticisms of the Harvard criteria. Jørgensen, Jørgensen, and Rosenklint (1973, pp. 363f.) admit to reservations concerning the four Harvard criteria for irreversible coma. (1) Total unawareness of externally applied stimuli. Unawareness is not an objectively recordable parameter, since (a) a patient may appear to react even if no cerebral function is present, and (b) no response does not prove unawareness of the stimulus. (2) Absent spontaneous respiration. This can only be demonstrated if the ventilator is turned off, an action not justifiable until all other signs of brain function have ceased. (3) Absent reflexes. Absence of cranial nerve reflexes is essential to diagnosis of brain death whereas spinal reflexes may be preserved with no cerebral function. Other reflex movements are reported in brain-dead patients (p. 363). (4) Flat EEG. The Harvard criterion (amplitude less than 5 μV for ten to twenty consecutive minutes) is said to be inadequate because cortical activity with an amplitude of 2–5 μV occurring with intervals of fifteen to twenty minutes has been observed. With these reservations however, Jørgensen, Jørgensen, and Rosenklint (1973, p. 364) subscribe to the Harvard criteria, and they mention other studies that cite criteria of hypothermia and abrupt fall in blood pressure.

Many of the ensuing developments, while they also initially appear to be criticisms of the Harvard criteria, are really attempts to improve or supplement them, or to stress different aspects of the criteria and shift priorities.

A set of criteria formulated by the University of Minnesota Health Sciences Center places more emphasis on clinical judgement than does the Harvard criteria, and does not require an EEG reading. Five criteria (given here in abbreviated form) are set out: (1) no spontaneous movement; (2) no spontaneous respiration when tested for a period of four minutes at a time; (3) absence of brain stem reflexes; (4) all three above remain unchanged for twenty-four hours; (5) the processes responsible for (1)–(4) are irreparable with presently available means. Mohandas and Chou (1971, p. 212) contend "in patients with known but irrepairable intracranial lesions,

determination of brain death can be based on clinical judgement."
They allow however (p. 217) that use of the EEG is "both useful and
necessary in unusual circumstances where the nature of the injury is
known." It is important, though, to note (p. 216) that they are
thinking of clinical judgement by a competent neurosurgeon.

Another report weighs criteria somewhat differently and stresses
caution in the use of EEG findings. Juul-Jensen (1970, p. 14) rules
that a patient may only be a potential organ donor if five criteria are
met. (1) Documented irreversible brain damage. The nature,
extent, and course of the cerebral lesion must be known. (2) Deep
coma. This entails no response to external stimuli, a neurological
examination for absence of various reflexes, no spontaneous respiration, blood pressure maintained only by vasopressor drugs, and
absence of response to atropine evidenced by no change in cardiac
rhythm. (3) Caloric test. Irrigation of one ear with cold water affects
the deviation of the eyes toward the irrigated ear (p. 12). (4) Isoelectric EEG. The EEG should be interpreted by "a doctor with
wide experience in clinical neurophysiology who must also subject
the patient to a clinical examination" (p. 14). Recording should be
at least thirty minutes. Flat EEG is a *sine qua non* but can never stand
alone. (5) Findings must be constant in two recordings at an interval
of at least twenty-four hours.

So far we do not appear to have deviated too far from the basic
outline of the Harvard criteria, but more radical departures can be
found.

European Developments: Cerebral Blood Circulation

One most interesting development has been the introduction of the
additional criterion of absence of cerebral blood circulation. The set
of criteria proposed in 1966 by G. P. J. Alexandre of Belgium
includes: (1) complete mydriasis (extreme dilatation of the pupil of
the eye); (2) complete absence of reflexes; (3) complete absence of
spontaneous ventilation during five minutes without ventilatory
support; (4) falling blood pressure; (5) flat electroencephalogram.
Two criteria are added by Revilliard, noted by Harp (1974, p. 392):
(1) interruption of blood flow to the brain as determined by angio-

graphy;[2] and (2) absence of tachycardia in response to atrophine. The French Surgical Society uses the term *coma dépassé* (beyond coma) for patients meeting these criteria. Designed to meet problems of organ transplantation, these criteria omit the twenty-four hour delay of the Harvard criteria. Harp (1974, p. 392) reports that the following authorities report criteria similar to those of Alexandre and Revilliard: Craaford of Stockholm, Ewing of Melbourne, Hamburger of Paris, and Schuster of Mainz.

The Allegheny Committee of 1969 (Allegheny Ad Hoc Committee on Tissue Transplantation of the Institute of Forensic Science of the Duquesne University School of Law) combines the Harvard and Alexandre-Revilliard criteria: (1) absence of all brain and spinal reflexes; (2) isoelectric EEG; (3) falling blood pressure; (4) all to be present for two hours. Two physicians other than the physician of the organ recipient are required for certification. A fuller account is given by Wecht (1969) and Harp (1974, p. 393).

The Belgian article of Jacquy, Lacoge, and Mouawad (1974) postulates three sets of criteria: (1) clinical—the classical French diagnosis of Mollaret and Goulon of *coma dépassé*; (2) electroencephalographic—isoelectric (flat, null) EEG; (3) circulatory—absence of circulation in the brain—tested by bilateral carotid angiography, or in case of doubt, by vertebral angiography.

Jørgensen, Jørgensen, and Rosenklint (1973) report that a study of forty-two patients *in extremis* shows that brain death (irreversible cessation of all brain function) may be presumed if cranial nerve reflexes and EEG activity are absent, adding that the assumption is supported when cerebral perfusion pressure is below 10 mm Hg. Third, death may be documented when no brain circulation can be demonstrated twice at an interval of twenty minutes.

Van Till (1975, p. 139) outlines three "schools" of diagnosing death. The Anglo-American school comprises essentially the Harvard criteria except that, according to *Lancet* (1974) one hour instead of twenty-four is the period for re-evaluation. The French diagnosis is based on irreversible *coma dépassé*: the requirements are the Harvard criteria plus "loss of spontaneous regulation of temperature and blood pressure and an isoelectric EEG for at least twenty-four hours." The Austro-German diagnosis requires irrefutable proof of brain

2. Angiography is a method of determining cerebral blood flow by means of observation by photography of the course of a dye injected through an artery that flows through the brain.

death in addition to irreversible *coma dépassé*. She cites Krösl and
Scherzer (1973), reporting that such proof is obtainable "only from
bilateral serial angiography of the internal carotid and vertebral
arteries in the brain." What is required is a negative angiogram for
more than fifteen minutes (except in the case of younger persons or
where the history indicates the possibility of apparent death). Brain
death is characterized as "irreversible cessation of all functions of
the brain." Angiography is a test for blood circulation. As Van Till
summarizes, the French school is more careful than the Anglo-
American, but the German school clinches the diagnosis by requiring
proof of a fact that is incompatible with the existence of brain
function (Van Till, 1975, p. 140).

These developments suggest some controversy concerning the use
of the EEG and angiography as criteria for brain death. Indeed, a
statement issued by the Conference of Medical Royal Colleges and
their Faculties in the United Kingdom (1976) reports that it is
widely accepted that electroencephalography is not necessary for
diagnosing brain death. The statement adds that the EEG has its
principal uses at earlier stages of care, where the original diagnosis
is in doubt. Nor are other investigations such as angiography or
cerebral blood flow tests said to be required. However, two important
areas of debate in the methodology of brain death diagnosis are
emphasized. First, it is vital to exclude patients who have received
large doses of cerebral or autonomic depressants. Second, the carbon
dioxide level in the arterial blood is a critical factor in evaluating lack
of respiration as an indication of brain death. If the carbon dioxide
level is low, there may be no respiration for five or six minutes until
the level rises to a point to actuate the physiological drive to the
respiratory center. (This point was drawn to the attention of the
author by a British physician.)

The statement separates the various considerations into three
parts. In the first part, conditions for considering diagnosis of brain
death are given. Three conditions must jointly coexist. (1) *The patient
is deeply comatose.* Depressant drugs, hypothermia, and metabolic or
endocrine disturbances must be excluded as possible causes. (2) *The
patient is being maintained on a ventilator because spontaneous respiration had
previously become inadequate or had ceased altogether.* Relaxants and other
drugs should be excluded as possible causes. (3) *There should be no
doubt that the patient's condition is due to irremediable structural brain
damage. The diagnosis of a disorder which can lead to brain death should have*

been fully established. The point is made here that while diagnosis may be obvious in some cases, in others considerable clinical observation and investigation may be required. In the second part of the statement, six tests for confirming brain death are given: (a) fixed pupils, (b) no corneal reflex, (c) no eye movements when ice water is poured into the ear, (d) no motor responses following stimulation of a somatic area, (e) no gag reflex, (f) no respiratory movements when the patient is disconnected from the ventilating machine, provided the carbon dioxide level in the blood is adequate. On (f) it is required that if blood gas analysis is not available, the alternative procedure should be to supply the ventilator with pure oxygen for ten minutes, then with 5 percent carbon dioxide in the oxygen for five minutes, then to disconnect the ventilator for ten minutes while delivering oxygen by catheter into the trachea. In the third part, it is of interest to note, in light of the controversies on the Harvard criteria, that the interval for repetition of testing is said to be a matter for medical judgement. The interval between tests could therefore be highly variable, and might be as long as twenty-four hours.

Critiques of the Electroencephalograph

Some discussion of the weighting of the value of EEG findings has occurred. The findings of Juul-Jensen (1970) show the significance of a isoelectric EEG—in his study only one out of seventy-two unconscious patients with isoelectric EEG survived—but, it is added, the EEG is of value only when accompanied by other clinical data. The most important criterion is said to be knowledge of the type, extent, and course of the cerebral lesion in a potential donor. There are documented cases of survival after an isoelectric EEG reading, and Juul-Jensen (1970, pp. 49ff.) rebuts the significance of these for his criteria, since in each case some *other* criterion of brain death was not met.

The Robinson editorial (1972) suggests that undue emphasis has been placed on the EEG and that the clinical criteria of Mohandas and Chou (1971) without EEG are adequate. Robinson (1975) reports that the issue has become much simpler medically, and that brain death can be assessed by any doctor without laboratory equipment by means of the following criteria: (1) no spontaneous respiration during five minutes off the ventilator; (2) fixed (usually dilated) pupils unreactive to light; (3) brain stem reflexes absent; (4) no motor response to pain in the facial area. Thus EEG or angiography findings do not, according to Robinson (1975), over-ride these clinical criteria. It is stressed, however, that the previous history is all-important. We should note in connection with (2) that, as Jørgensen, Jørgensen, and Rosenklint (1973) observed in connection with the Harvard criteria, taking the patient off the ventilator is presumably not justifiable until brain death has been independently established.

An editorial in *Lancet* (1974) confirms the University of Minnesota findings in its suggestion that insistence on an isoelectric EEG as an essential condition of brain death puts an unfair responsibility on electroencephalographers, yet is equally unfair "to experienced clinicians, who may know from the whole clinical picture that a patient will not recover, yet may be inhibited from acting accordingly." Given the development of techniques for diagnosis of cessation of cerebral blood flow, a different approach from the Harvard framework may seem to be developing.

We hasten to add that there is a vast literature on the value of the EEG machine as a diagnostic tool in this area, and we will not attempt by any means to do justice to this technical issue here. We do need to note however that qualified authors have expressed reservations and qualifications about certain aspects of EEG diagnosis, and that alternative methods are available that may help to supplement the EEG techniques.

The Role of Angiography

Van Till (1975) stresses that criteria for death should be conclusive,[3] and that the method that seems to be most conclusive is that of demonstration of absence of blood flow in the brain. Braunstein, Korein, et al. (1973) stress a parameter additional to clinical and EEG findings that can increase the reliability and decrease the time required to diagnose brain death, namely, the absence of cerebral circulation. They report (p. 759) "the development of a safe and simple bedside method of demonstrating cerebral circulatory deficit using a portable dual scintillation probe system coupled to ratemeters and chart recorders to detect and display the passage of an

3. Note also the remark of Harp (1974, p. 395): "the chief determinant . . . must clearly be a certainty of hopelessness."

intravenously injected radioisotopic bolus of technetium 99m per-technetate (Tc 99m O_4) through the cerebral circulation." If clinical criteria are met and an isoelectric EEG is present, a portable radio-isotopic blood flow test showing no cerebral circulation for a duration of one hour might be sufficient to diagnose brain death.

Juul-Jensen (1970, p. 51) states that tests for cerebral blood flow are useful supplementary diagnostic extensions but that the central point remains the clinical evaluation made by an experienced neurosurgeon. Repeated clinical examinations are also stressed. Even if tests for cerebral blood flow may be regarded as highly reliable indicators of cessation of brain activity, such tests may not be needed in every instance, where other indicators are equally reliable.

Van Till (1975, p. 139) reports that the Austro-German diagnosis of 1969 outlined by Penin and Kaufer (1969 and 1973) requires "irrefutable proof of brain death" in addition to irreversible *coma dépassé*. This is diagnosed by "bilateral serial angiography of the internal carotid and vertebral arteries in the brain." Juul-Jensen (1970, p. 11) agrees that pan-arteriography may be used to demon-strate absence of cerebral blood flow in transplantation donors, but that this will "rarely be necessary, as the experienced clinician easily recognizes how the vital functions gradually deteriorate." (He is thinking of cases where the type, extent, and course of the cerebral lesion in the donor are established.)

Walker (1974, pp. 190f.) gives a set of clinical neurologic criteria on which "there is practically universal agreement": (1) a comatose patient unresponsive to painful stimulus; (2) paralysis of respiratory effort and consequent artificial ventilation; (3) bilateral dilated and fixed pupils; (4) absent corneal reflexes; (5) lack of vestibular response in a caloric test, as more fully outlined by Juul-Jensen (1970, p. 12); (6) absence of tendon reflexes and of superficial abdominal and plantar reflexes. According to Walker, however, these criteria are almost sufficient, but electroencephalographic and angiographic tests must be met also. Some metabolic methods, and other methods, including the insertion of brain probes, are mentioned as "final criteria," even though the latter methods require a minor surgical operation and may therefore be found objectionable.

Walker (1974, p. 200) points out that the determination of brain death has a dual role in medical decision making. It may serve the purpose of instigating a total resuscitative program or of stopping resuscitative measures. But it may be questioned whether the criteria should be the same in each case. At certain junctures, a variety of factors, not all primarily medical, may influence the decision one way or the other. An early cerebral angiogram might allow the clinician to confirm or eliminate the possibility of a treatable condition. If the condition is not treatable, the physician may be less inclined to prolong the coma by chemical or mechanical aids. Here, the customary criteria, perhaps refined by electrocardiogram, determine the moment of death. But if permission is given for organ removal, it must be determined that the heart has stopped beating.

On the other side, Walker continues, if findings indicate that therapy may effectively prolong life, "the best and latest resuscitative methods must be employed" (p. 200). If therapy fails, criteria of brain death may again be assessed. If organ transplantation is being considered, Walker urges a "hypercritical attitude toward the determinants of death" to safeguard the patient's rights. Here, additional criteria over and above the clinical and electroencephalographic tests may identify "more precisely and more conclusively" the moment of death. Four *final criteria* are given: (1) complete absence on neurological examination of evidence of (a) movement, (b) responsiveness, (c) respiratory effort, and (d) cranial nerve reflexes; (2) flat EEG for thirty minutes even when the record is run at twice the standard gain; (3) cerebral oxygen consumption below 10 percent of normal or angiographic evidence of failure of intercranial circulation; (4) as final confirmation, absence of bioelectric activity in the thalamus, as determined by a depth electrode (Walker, 1974, p. 201). Walker concludes that until the time comes when society looks at brain death the way it now looks at cardiac death, it remains desirable that, if the brain alone is dead, the physician should share the final decision with other physicians who must consider "the informed advice of legal, religious, and sociological colleagues." Hence the neuroscientist alone should not bear responsibility for determination of death where vital organs still function.

According to the report of Ingvar et al. (1974), brain death can be diagnosed "without aortocranial angiography, purely on the basis of clinical neurological findings and EEC examinations, provided the cause is known." The report explains that in brain death there is no blood flow to the central nervous structures above the spinal segment C1. *Brain death* is here defined as "an irreversible cessation of function of all cerebral structures, including the cerebellum and brain stem down to spinal section C1. (See the comments in Van Till,

1975, on the importance of characterizing brain death as total irreversibility of function of the whole brain.)[4] According to Ingvar et al. (1974, p. 530), brain death is caused "either by a primary intracranial disorder, such as traumatic brain injury, intracranial hemorrhage, an expanding lesion, etc., or by general cerebral anoxia following, e.g., asphyxia or cardiac arrest." Both causes lead to brain swelling and pressure that in turn leads to cessation of intracranial blood circulation. At least, the report states, this sequence of events is the "main pathogenic factor" in brain death. Angiography is said to be "the method of choice" in proving absence of circulation by Ingvar et al. (1974, p. 531), and can diagnose brain death with certainty even where the cause is unknown, but where the cause is known, certain diagnosis is possible by means of clinical findings and EEG examination alone, according to the report.

Summary

Our impression of these proposals does not support the hypothesis of the disparate collection of opposed or contradictory "definitions of death" that is sometimes popularly supposed to exist.[5] Rather we have what seems to be an orderly development of attempts to improve on the previous attempts by weighting various factors differently or by supplementing previous findings. The "new" criteria do not entail rejection of the traditional criteria, but rather adding special criteria to meet new circumstances. It is universally acknowledged that the EEG is a useful and important development, but the importance of supportive clinical criteria and the role of the physician's judgement (particularly that of the neurosurgeon) is stressed in using the EEG. The tests for cerebral blood flow may, in turn, be seen as an adjunct to the EEG and other criteria rather than as a replacement or alternative.

Van Till (1975) sees in the European development of cerebral blood flow criteria a greater emphasis on irrefutable, conclusive proof of diagnosis than in the Anglo-American school of thought. Perhaps this is so, but the difference need not be an irresolvable one or clash of principles. Rather, these developments might only tend

4. The reader might recall the notes in chapter I on brain death.
5. See, for example, Kennedy (1971).

to show that tests for cerebral blood flow can be used to supplement the other criteria in special cases where diagnosis is more difficult or problematic. Nothing in this chapter rules out the interpretation that the literature exhibits an orderly development of movement towards greater certainty of diagnosis through technical improvements of existing techniques and development of new techniques to supplement the existing methods. Given our awareness of the respective roles of definitions and criteria developed in chapter II, it seems implausible that any suggestion of conceptual pluralism need be required exclusively on the basis of the developments outlined in chapter III. On the other hand, in many instances the new criteria have been intended and may be taken to be replacements or successors for the traditional clinical criteria in certain instances. Advances in medical technology have changed the medico-philosophical context in such a way that new criteria and new methods of diagnosis are necessary. Although it may fairly be said that these new criteria began as ancillary methods of clinical diagnosis, nevertheless they have passed into the defining context of death itself by their effect on our thinking about death at the conceptual level. The question then remains open whether a conceptual pluralism or monism is the sounder interpretation of these diagnostic developments. The point is that the level of diagnostic criteria cannot compel us to infer to the correctness of one or the other conclusions at the conceptual level. To study the logic of inferences of this type we need to examine the concept of death, at a conceptual level of adequate philosophical and analytical clarity, in order to try to determine what it is medical technology attempts to diagnose. We now turn to an analysis of the concept of death.

Chapter IV

Conditions for Defining Death

As a background to attempting to provide an analysis of death at the conceptual level, we here set out some assumptions and a set of adequacy conditions in which to frame a definition or theory. These conditions will inevitably seem arbitrary to some readers. But on the other hand, we hope they will be intuitively compelling to others, and without some such set of guidelines, the analysis is without a "target." As Carnap (1950) points out, an analysis must have some set of conditions of success, however roughly formulated, if a charge of vacuity is to be countered.

Secular and Religious Assumptions

For whatever historical reasons, the philosophical logic of death from a secular point of view has simply not been explored in recent times in any systematic way. Here we draw a contrast between the *secular conception of death*, total and irreversible extinction of consciousness and sensation, including discontinuation of actual survival of the individual personality, and the *religious conception of death* that postulates actual survival of the individual personality and continuation of *post mortem* consciousness and sensation.[1] Both views deserve study, since both are widely accepted, but the secular view in particular contains inconsistencies and paradoxes (as we will show) to the extent that it may seem scarcely coherent. We restrict chapters IV and V to an investigation of the underlying logic of the secular view by philosophical and semantical methods. In chapter VI, a basis for a similar

1. Historically influential varieties of both conceptions are chronicled by Choron (1963).

set of guidelines is constructed as a prolegomenon to an inquiry into the religious conception of death.[2]

The object of this chapter is to contribute to the clarification of some conceptual quirks in the secular view of death wherein death is said to entail total, permanent extinction of consciousness. In our increasingly secular age, despite much recent interest in euthanasia and other death-related problems, many significant immediate logical consequences of this view remain obscure and paradoxical, and it is to the ancient Stoics and Epicureans that we must turn for the most determined precedent attempts to cope with these arcane inconsistencies. As in that early period of intense scientific secularism, ordinary secular attitudes today towards death constitute a classical case of cognitive dissonance. Fear of *nothing* seems somehow unjustifiable or inappropriate, yet who other than the convinced believer can deny awareness of that anxiety, *timor mortis*, the horror of the abyss, thanatophobia, fear of the plunge into darkness. Towards understanding the underlying logic of this dissonance-producing belief-conflict, two broad secular theoretical overviews of death will be outlined, and against this background the question will be posed whether and how death can be consistently understood as a misfortune. Focusing on this latter question in particular will function as a dialectical device, a basis for exploring more fundamental puzzles: How can we understand the logic of cognitively null states? How can we understand transition into the null state? How can an individual who no longer exists be the victim of a misfortune? Posing the question of death as misfortune will reveal inconsistencies and conceptual intransigencies in the logic and language of death whose exploration may, we hope, serve as a contribution towards better understanding the foundations of the metaphysics and ethics of death.

Negation, Event, or Transformation?

Death may vaguely be thought of as an event that takes place in or at the end of the life of a person. But if death is an event, it is a unique "event," as we can see by making a number of elementary observations. First, once it occurs, it lasts for ever—that is, death has

2. See Choron (1963, Book II), Hick (1957, pp. 154ff.), Hick (1968, chs. 4 and 5), Young (1970), and Clark (1971).

infinite duration—otherwise it might not be death but merely a disorder that has occurred if the possibility of reversal obtains at all.[3] Second, death, if thought of as "momentary," as opposed to dying, does not take any time at all to occur, unless perhaps it occurs in one instant of time. That is, a natural way to think of death is as an instantaneous transformation from a finite state (life) into a permanent state (?), death. Even this conception reveals an ambiguity: is death the point of transformation, or the everlasting segment that begins after this point? Perhaps the most natural analogy might be to think of life as a line, drawn from left to right (proceeding from the past to the future), where death includes a point on the line plus the segment of the line that extends indefinitely to the right.

Yet often death is spoken of as an "event" that takes a definite but extended stretch of time to occur, rather than as an instantaneous or momentary state-change. Expressions like "He died slowly" and so forth suggest an event that takes place in an interval, even if the interval may often, or even characteristically, be rather short. Thus perhaps a line, marked off on a longer line might be the appropriate geometric analogy.

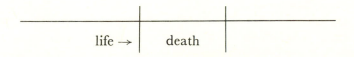

This is not quite right however, in that it suggests that there is some third state after death, which seems questionable on the secular hypothesis—unless of course death has an irreducibly dual aspect. That is, it might be thought of as initially an event that, at some point becomes a permanent state. The intuition here underlying either conception, that of event or state-change, following Kastenbaum and Aisenberg (1972, p. 113) is that an essentially physical,

3. *See* Van Till (1975, pp. 133f.), Kastenbaum and Aisenberg (1972, p. 113), and chapter X below.

objective, underlying reference point underlies our death-related thoughts, behaviors, and experiences. Yet the notion of death as a "state" or "event" is peculiar because it is permanent, once actualized, and because it may be seen as a "negative state," as the negation of life rather than as something positive in itself. Third, death is in certain respects a "null state," for on the *secular conception* death is widely thought to be the utter extinction of all consciousness, the utter cancellation of all states that an individual can pass through. Moreover, how could death be a state that an individual is in, if that individual has ceased to exist? On the *theological conception*, where death is a transformation from one kind of individual to another, or the survival of the same individual in a different form, it is easier to justify the language of states and events. But on the secular hypothesis, it verges on fallacy to characterize death as a positive state, but approaches obscurity to talk about null states or transitions into the void.

Many of the misfortunes that befall us can be understood as misfortunes, disasters, harms, evils, or calamities, only in virtue of their constituting or causing a state-change in the unfortunate individual. Consider Nagel's case (1970, p. 76) of a normal man reduced by an accident to the state of a three-year-old child. His life-history can be divided into two adjacent segments, neither state being essentially tragic or unfortunate in itself. What is unfortunate lies in the disparity between what he is—the mental equivalent of a three-year-old—and what he could have been—a normal man, perhaps sensitive, intelligent, and dignified, who might have undergone a wide range of experiences, thoughts, and emotions. Now take the case of death. Epicurus was quite right in observing that neither state—the life-state before death or the totally irrevocably unconscious death-state—is a misfortune if considered solely in itself. When we are alive we are not dead yet, and when we are dead we presumably don't know the difference anyway. The misfortune, if there is one, must lie in the transition. Only if the two states are juxtaposed and compared in some way does the element of misfortune become manifest.

Yet if death, like some other misfortunes, is to be thought of as a binary relation on ordered pairs of states, it is unique among these misfortunes, for the second member of the pair is the null state. For death is not a state at all on the secular hypothesis—it is *le néant*, the abyss, nothing, the utter cancellation of all states that an individual can pass through. If it is a "state," it is a peculiar one, being permanent once actualized. Moreover, how could it be a "state" that an individual is in, if the individual has ceased to exist? Viewing death as a positive state is tantamount to committing a kind of fallacy of misplaced concreteness if, as Van Evra (1971) would have us believe, death is best understood negatively as the limit of life. Thus the really profound challenge of Epicurus' remark emerges. How can we understand the idiom of the null state? How can we understand transition into the void? For otherwise death yields no misfortune.

One way to try to avoid the apparent fallacy of hypostatizing death is to think of it as an essentially negative concept. If we could think of life as a set, a set of states or events for example, we could think of death as the complement of that set. The latter set would include all states or events outside the life of a given individual. This set would be too wide, however, for it would include the states or events before that individual was born (at which time he was not yet dead, but also not yet alive). This difficulty seems to indicate that death is an essentially temporal concept—the notion of "after" is required to provide even a minimally adequate characterization.

So far we have been thinking of death primarily as that segment of the line that is to the right of the transformation point (including possibly also the point itself). But it is also natural to think of death as the transformation between the two sets but also containing both sets. Accordingly, we might think of an ordered pair of sets, $\langle S_1, S_2 \rangle$ where death is thought of as a state-change, comprising both states. This is a somewhat expanded view of death, since death encompasses the left-most part of the line (life) as well as the right segment. This binary view could be combined with the view of death as complement, so that death could be characterized as an ordered pair $\langle S_1, \bar{S}_1 \rangle$ (again, some temporal assumptions need to be presumed). Later we will see that it helps considerably to explain how death is sometimes thought to be an object of negative value (evil) if we can view it as a state-change rather than simply as a unary state. The binary idiom by no means altogether resolves our earlier problems, however, for we are still obliged to explain what the second element of the pair consists in, or if it is simply the complement of the first, what *it* consists in.

The above considerations sketch out a very rough and vague model of the secular conception of death by suggesting the following adequacy conditions for what we might consider a *standard* or *traditional* secular concept of death.

1. *D* is a null state.
2. *D* occurs instantaneously.
3. *D* is permanent and irreversible.
4. *D* postdates, but does not antedate, a lifetime.

None of these conditions is as clear as we might like, but each of them is sufficiently essential to the broad secular notion of death that if one condition were to fail to obtain in relation to a state, *D*, then the conception of death represented by *D* would be non-standard.[4] The second condition is perhaps the most questionable, as stated, since, as we have seen, there may be an aspect of duration involved in death, though how this aspect fits in, in view of the third condition seems highly problematic.

Levels of Analysis

We must now clearly distinguish again between the question of the *meaning* of death, with which we have heretofore been occupied in a preliminary way, and the related but distinct question related to chapter III of how we *know* that an individual is dead—the latter is an epistemic (knowledge) question. The distinction may be illustrated by the discussion of Kastenbaum and Aisenberg (1972, pp. 113ff.) of the third condition. As they put it, "Death endures endlessly, without limit in time. Death would not be death if it did not last forever." If we were to interpret the third as an epistemic condition, then irrefutable determination of death could not be carried out until there remained no possibility of observation to the contrary: he looks dead now, he has looked dead for the last hour, the last day, the last week, but it is theoretically possible that next week he will give new evidence of life (Kastenbaum and Aisenberg, 1972, 115). Kastenbaum and Aisenberg ask: Under what general conditions could death be certified as permanent, and hence really death? The condition might be that there is an observer who survives for all time, or for whom time is irrelevant. Now quite

---

4. Kastenbaum and Aisenberg (1972, pp. 124ff.) discuss some interesting arguments for challenging our "bias" that death is the ending or absence of life. Thus we do not wish to rule out that under some conceivable circumstances one or more of the adequacy conditions might be rejected on reasonable grounds.

clearly, the postulation of such extravagant assumptions reduces to absurdity the identification of the third as an epistemic condition. Questions pertaining to our means of knowing whether it obtains, and the degree to which we can reasonably be confident that it obtains, are quite distinct from the purely semantical question of whether it is essential to the meaning of "death." The two kinds of questions are, of course, intimately related, but it is important to separate them in theory if we are to avoid needless controversy and pointless confusion. We have seen in chapter II that this kind of confusion is inherent in much of the current idiom of "defining" and "redefining" death: a list of physical indications of how we know death has occurred does not necessarily by any means constitute an adequate analysis of the meaning of death.

Death and Consciousness

We turn to some epistemic questions. There is an analogy between some epistemic properties of death and the classical philosophical problem of other minds.[5] My way of knowing that I have a pain may be quite different in principle from any way I have of knowing that you have a pain. I have "privileged access" to my own private mental states. In the same way, my death is my own and cannot be undergone by you as the subject of it. But the analogy is inverted by the epistemic vacuity of death on the secular conception. I cannot experience my own being-dead, but you, as an observer, can witness my death or being-dead. Thus on the secular hypothesis there is an "unverifiability" aspect of death. My death is something about which I can have no direct personal knowledge by observation—it is, so to speak, epistemically out of my range altogether. Thus someone who is inclined to identify knowledge with observation may conclude that it is pointless to attempt to gain any knowledge about death at all, that for lack of *data* such conjectures are mere empty speculation. We need to be careful here, however. While there is an important element of epistemic inaccessibility that is characteristic of death, it need not follow that we can know nothing whatever about death. To return to the analogy of other minds—I do not have direct access to your mental states, but it may be very useful for me

5. See also the remarks of Kluge (1975, pp. 145ff.).

to make certain reasonable inferences about them, and to evaluate these inferences against the evidence that I do have that is relevant to them.

One significant consequence of the first-hand observational epistemic inaccessibility of death is that, given widely prevalent views, one seems to be forced to decide, in the face of lack of any direct relevant evidence, between the secular and the religious conception. The situation is not symmetrical, however. The secular hypothesis might plausibly cite indirect data (the inanimacy of the dead) whereas the religious conception appears to accept and in-corporate these data into a larger overview that includes survival on a different level.[6] What asymmetry there is may be accounted for by the greater importance which secular thinkers on this question have traditionally attached to empirical data.[7] The classical account of this epistemic dichotomy, that of Kant in the "Transcendental Dialectic" of the *Critique of Pure Reason*, postulates a symmetrical antinomy between the religious and secular hypotheses and argues that since both views are under-determined by empirical data, the decision is not one that can be made by pure reason. In other writings, however, Kant was to reject the symmetry by arguing that practical or moral considerations bear on the religious hypothesis. The relationships between the secular and religious views could be made more intelligible by an exploration of the question "What are the limits of our knowledge of death?" in a Kantian spirit.[8]

Thus if we consider the various conjectures that are traditionally offered—the Socratic view that death affects the physical organism only and not the soul, the Aristotelian conjecture that *noûs*, the ability to reason, is a divine element in men and may not perish entirely in death, the Epicurean view that death is accompanied by total lack of sensation, the Stoic view that the individual soul is destroyed in death, the New Testament view that the spiritual man is reborn through a gift of God, the Cartesian view that the soul is distinct from the body and does not disintegrate in death, and so

6. But Choron (1963) discusses these matters more fully.

7. My account here is much oversimplified, but more adequate elucidation is given in the following accounts: Hick (1957 and 1968), Young (1970), and Clarke (1971).

8. I will not pursue these highly controversial questions here, merely wishing to indicate what I think some of the philosophical problems are, and how they have an epistemic flavor.

forth[9]—it is highly problematic to suggest that there is some central disagreement running through them that any straightforward set of empirical data directly bears on. And as a matter of fact, each of these views is related to a broad philosophical theory of *life* or *man* that does not stand or fall in any obvious way on any well-circumscribed set of observations concerning death. For an attempt to work towards a theory of this type, see Fletcher (1973). About the best one can say is that those who take different points of view interpret the evidence differently. Despite these very real basic disagreements of point of view, there are, of course, certain biological, psychological, legal, medical, and philosophical questions also, that can be investigated in an objective way. We can investigate our attitudes towards death, we can investigate the logical consequences of adopting various assumptions about death, even if the assumptions are not themselves known to be true or false. We can investigate moral or legal questions about death without being dogmatic or apologetic. We can even, I am suggesting, study metatheoretical, epistemological questions concerning the limits of our knowledge in these matters. Within limits, some objective knowledge is possible, even if it is not the kind of knowledge we might hope for.

Death is often paradigmatically connected with loss of consciousness, of awareness, of sensation, just as life is often associated with the presence of these mentalistic properties. The force of their association in western thought is easy to appreciate, and I think that to some extent this accounts for the plausibility of the concept of brain death, insofar as the brain is connected with higher-order conscious activities. This element of consciousness obviously plays an important role in adequacy condition 1, and we will return to it in chapter V.

Who is Dead?

A logical difficulty inherent in the secular conception of death is prompted by the observation that according to this view the dead no

9. The reader is referred to Choron (1963) for a detailed account of these theories. It has been pointed out to me that Epicurus may not exclusively have confined himself to the view of death as a state of existence without sensation, even though that view represents the general Epicurean position. W. J. Oates in *The Stoic and Epicurean Philosophers* (p. 10) quotes Epicurus as saying " . . . nay more, whatever portions of the soul may perish too, when that which enclosed it is removed either in whole or in part, if the soul continues to exist at all, it will retain sensation."

longer exist as individuals. But how can we truly say, for example, that Socrates is dead if there is no individual, *Socrates*, who is dead? Or, to take another example, if I kill you, how can what I have done constitute a crime if there is no victim, no individual against whom a crime was allegedly committed? To put it another way, if I kill you, then on the secular conception it appears that what I have done is to cause you to vanish altogether (at least as an individual, although your corpse may remain). This bizarre consequence has some serious philosophical implications, for it does not appear to allow us to speak of the dead. In so doing, on the secular hypothesis, we speak about *nothing*. But as a matter of brute linguistic fact, we do speak about the dead, and we must, if we are to make any kind of coherent sense of apparently intelligible legal and ethical assertions about death.

One way to attempt to restore consistency between the secular hypothesis and these segments of the language of death might be to argue that when we assert "Socrates is dead" we really mean that the individual that was Socrates is now dead. He no longer exists as an individual, but at one time he did exist, and that individual is dead. (It is easy to see how any assumption of continued existence of someone not alive might be anathema to a secular theorist.) This seems more accurate, but still not wholly satisfactory. For take this "x" that was Socrates (the individual that was Socrates but is now dead). We speak of this individual, "x," now, and so it is accurate in a way to say that this "x" must be postulated as being in existence now even though it is not something that is Socrates but merely something that was Socrates. In other words, we seem to need a point of reference, "x," of which it is true now that "x" has the property of being dead and consequently has the property of being something that was, at one time, alive. But what is this "x"? Not Socrates, certainly not the live Socrates, and presumably not a ghost of Socrates. Quite simply, this "x" is something-that-was-Socrates, a temporally extended reference point extrapolated from the real, existent person Socrates who lived long ago, a reference point that allows us to talk about (the late) Socrates now even though he no longer exists.[10]

The problem with "x" is that, for one reason or another, it is fatally easy to get it mixed up with the actual Socrates. This "x"

10. The reader might look to Prior (1967) for a more sophisticated and detailed account of the logic of these types of points of temporal reference.

(the dead Socrates) is merely a possible Socrates and is by no means capable of carrying on in a Socrates-like manner or of doing anything at all. But believers in personal survival, who are prone to see this "x" as "the thin edge of the wedge," may be given to making much of any resemblance between the living Socrates and his futurized extension, possible-Socrates. Needless to add, Epicureans, Stoics, and other opponents of survival in any form, are likely to view "x" with hostility and suspicion. There is little danger of squeezing in sleight-of-hand proofs of immortality, however, if we remember that the "x," the possible Socrates, refers only to the individual that *was* Socrates. The use of a name, or piece of notation like "x," is merely a device that allows for some convenient tense-shifts and does not refer to actual persons in any form.

To sum up, it seems that in order to assure the consistency of the secular conception and its adequacy to the language of death in many important contexts, it is necessary to postulate the existence of certain temporal points of reference that may be thought of, in effect, as "possible (but definitely not actual) persons." This is a controversial step to take, and hard-headed empiricists and situational ethicists alike are sure to decry it as obscurantism. What are "possible persons" and "possible situations" in which these possible persons exist, and why should we proliferate such dubious entities at all? As others have pointed out, for example, Cresswell (1973), it is difficult to win over the skeptic by somehow convincing him that possible situations are metaphysically acceptable, or by trying to find an easy definition of a possible situation that is not open to objections. Rather one might assume that the language of possibilities is a permissible assumption with which we can see what we can do. It is fair to say that while the language of possible situations is accepted by many philosophers as a valuable linguistic tool of logic and analysis, others object to it for various reasons more fully discussed in Cresswell (1973, pp. 37ff.) and Rescher (1973). My feeling is that this language is now well established as a philosophical method, allows us to explore many new important domains, and is syntactically and semantically well understood and developed from a logical point of view as indicated in Hughes and Cresswell (1968). Most importantly, however, it seems to me that unless some idiom of modal logic like that represented by the language of possible situations is allowed, it is extremely hard to see how even the most elementary expressions of the language of death can be understood at all adequately so that some quotidien truths (or what are thought to be truths) can be preserved in an analysis. In my view, our remarks above on the person of Socrates confirm this thesis, and chapter V confirms it with redoubled force. For those who remain dubious about possible situations, perhaps the best we can hope for is a "wait and see" attitude. Perhaps I need not add that the question of possible worlds has been the subject of much intense recent discussion and controversy in philosophy, and not being able to deal in detail with all the issues it comprises, it must be accepted that my analysis has a provisional aspect. In support of the methodology of possible worlds however, I would cite the important results elsewhere of these methods in the work of Lewis (1973), Cresswell (1973), and Montague (1974).

Chapter V

The Superlimiting Theory of Death

We now proceed to develop a dual theory of death as experience and projection. Death is seen first, from within the viewpoint of the living person, and second, as a projection beyond actual experience or sensation.

Death As Limit

One way to characterize death is as the limit of experience, as the boundary or edge of life. On our earlier analogy of life as a line, death would be the point on the line such that all points to the left, and only those points, are within life. But how are we to understand the notion of a *limit?* Wittgenstein compared death as experiential limit to the limit of a field of vision: "Our life has no end in just the way in which our visual field has no limit" (Wittgenstein, 1961, 6.4311). What he meant by this aphoristic remark is presumably that a limit of experience is not itself within experience; visible limits are not themselves visible. Interestingly, this thesis can be justified by indirect proof: if the limit were itself within the visual field and was therefore a visible phenomenon, it could not possibly constitute the limit, since it would be itself within the limit of that visual field. By analogy, death as the limit of experience cannot be itself within experience. Of course my death can be experienced vicariously or indirectly by you, but my death cannot be within the range of my own personal experience.[1] Again, I can experience my own dying, but not my own death, where death is thought of as the limit, whereas dying is the terminal segment of life.

This Wittgensteinian analogy is extended by Van Evra (1971)

1. Epicurus' preference for a strongly empirical view was made quite plain in his famous remarks linking death with absence of sensation.

into a general conception of death. If death is outside experience, there are essential epistemic limitations on the concept of death. Contrary to what seems the prevalent existentialist view, we cannot have a direct awareness of death as a positive phenomenon. Van Evra introduces the mathematical concept of *limit*, a relation between two quantities such that one approaches the other without ever coinciding with it; for example, an asymptotic curve comes closer and closer to a line, but never actually touches it (except at infinity). Similarly, we move toward death throughout life, and our lives are ordered in experience in such a manner that they point towards death and progress towards death, but never actually reach death in experience.

It is interesting to note that the conception of death as the limit of experience is highly compatible with the ancient doctrines of Epicurus in the *Principal Doctrines II*: "Death is nothing to us; for what has been dissolved has no sensation, and what has no sensation is nothing to us." The Epicurean and Stoic arguments of this type are well known: death should not be feared, since it is not painful, simply because it is beyond experience altogether.

We return to thanatophobia later, but for the present it is useful to note one consequence in particular that is drawn by Van Evra from the conception of death as limit: "Conceiving of death as a function of life actually aids Epicurus' criticism by showing how talk of death can be so construed that the assumption of the existence of experienceless selves can be avoided" (Van Evra, 1971, p. 175). The significance of death is not as a state in itself, but rather as a device that orders life, just as a *function* orders the members of the series that are limited by it. This view of death thus allows death to be definable in terms of life, and therefore eliminates the need to postulate any entities beyond life—it is an essentially negative view of death, we might say. According to Van Evra, it is not the cessation of the ego we wish to avoid, but things which could be described as results of applying death as a functor—separation from friends, inability to attain goals, and so forth. According to the critical view of death as limit, cessation of the ego is simply out of our conceptual range altogether. This conception of death is an empirical and critical view—death is viewed from within life and experience, and is not something positive and actual in itself apart from experience—death is derivative from life, the limit of life. Thus the assumption of continuing, experienceless selves, the existence of points of reference (the "x" we spoke of in chapter IV), is to be avoided as simply incomprehensible or incoherent. This might gladden the heart of a hard-headed secular empiricist, but it also seems to leave us bereft of resources for explaining how statements like "Socrates is dead" are thought to be true, as we saw in chapter IV. Moreover, other problems are in store for the limiting conception.

The Superlimiting Conception

Even to strict exponents of the secular view, it may seem arbitrary to restrict ourselves to a language bound to categorical statements of moments in the life of an individual. Nagel (1970) argues that we can only understand death as a misfortune if we expand this restrictive approach and identify a person with his capabilities and possibilities in addition to what he actually is and does. Our belief that a death is tragic, evil, or otherwise open to negative evaluations seems often related to a belief that a person could have realized certain potentialities if he had not died at the time he did. That is, we need to take into account what a person could be or could have been, in addition to considering what he is or was. Nagel shows that the idea can be illustrated even without considering "experience-less selves" by considering the case of an intelligent person who receives a brain injury and is reduced to the mental condition of a contented baby. If we concentrate on the actuality of an oversized baby, there is no apparent misfortune. "He does not mind his condition. It is in fact the same condition he was in at the age of three months, except that he is bigger. If we did not pity him then, why pity him now; in any case, who is there to pity? The intelligent adult has disappeared, and for a creature like the one before us, happiness consists in a full stomach and a dry diaper" (Nagel, 1970, p. 76). The misfortune is only apparent if we consider the contrast between what he is, and what he could have been if the accident had not occurred. Nagel concludes that the view of death that restricts us to consideration only of the actual moments of life fails to do justice to the widespread and apparently reasonable belief that death is often, if not in some respects always, a misfortune. It is perhaps indicative of their identification of death with absence of sensation that the Stoics and Epicureans held the view widely thought paradoxical that it is completely irrational to fear death. For exclusively in terms of actual first-hand experience, it seems extremely difficult to make sense of speaking of death or the dead at all. What we cannot directly experience, we simply cannot understand. All such statements then become beyond the range of verification or even understanding. But in particular, statements about possible persons, of the kind outlined in chapter IV or of the kind proposed by Nagel, fall outside the range of the limiting conception of death. What is required to satisfy Nagel's requirement is a superlimiting conception of death that allows us to attribute properties to possible persons now dead without contravening the secular conception of death.

One kind of justification for the statement "His death was tragic," is often offered in the form, "If he had survived (for a given time) his continued life would have been worthwhile, valuable, etc." I will not try to argue that this line of justification or explanation of the belief that death is evil or tragic is the best or most central one, or indeed that it is the only legitimate line of argument. But I think it is fairly obvious that this line represents one important aspect of the widespread belief that death is sometimes, often, or perhaps even always, open to negative evaluation as an "evil" and the like. In defence of my own preoccupation with this theme however, I would like to point out that it has been explicated clearly and ably defended by L. W. Sumner, who writes "To die is (as we say) to lose one's life. Generally speaking, a loss is a bad thing to the extent that the item lost is a good thing. Losing a stutter, or losing one's fear of flying, or inches off one's waistline is not usually accounted an evil. Losing one's life must therefore be an evil when, and to the extent that, one's life is a good" (Sumner, 1976, pp. 157f.). We might call this line of thought the *deprivation thesis*. We find it also nicely stated by Nagel (1970, p. 74): "Clearly if death is an evil at all, it cannot be because of its positive features, but only because of what it deprives us of."

The form of the deprivation thesis is that of the counterfactual, "If so-and-so were the case, then such-and-such would be the case." The deprivation thesis presupposes that there can be a hypothetical situation or "possible world" (not the actual world) in which the dead person "survives" and in which properties of valuableness and worthwhileness are true to his hypothetical continued existence. As Sumner (1976, p. 158) put it, losses are future and possibility oriented: "Suppose that I own a fine watch for a year and then mislay it. What precisely have I lost? I cannot lose the year's possession and use of the watch, for that is in the past. What I have lost, then, is the use of the watch which I would have enjoyed had I continued to possess it." My loss pertains to a possible future. But what is the nature of these "hypothetical individuals" whose continued existence in a possible future is presupposed?

In speaking of death, what reference points are the properties of loss predicated to in such a possible situation? Not to the actual individual in question, for he is dead, but to the "individual" who could have survived, what we might call a "possible individual" (or hypothetical individual). Now this hypothetical individual of whom we speak will have to have certain properties to make our counterfactual meaningful. He will have to be very much like the actual individual up to the time of death of the actual individual, and also share certain essential characteristics beyond that point. He will, of course, not share all properties with his dead actual counterpart, since by hypothesis, he has survived. Where a line represents the actual situation, a divergent line suggests a hypothetical course of events that would have occurred if death had not occurred.

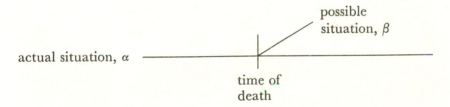

α represents what actually happened, but β represents what could have happened. In other words, β is simply an alternative possibility. The language of alternative possibilities seems essential to the fullest understanding of death, but is it a language that we can understand?

The Counterlimit Thesis

In accord with the superlimiting view, death may have a negative value just where the possible continuation of life has a positive value. The application of this value standard is particularly appropriate where the deceased possessed some otherwise promising potential talent or ability, as for example in the case of the tragic climbing death of the young mathematician, Herbrand. But the superlimiting view can also be applied to less paradigmatic cases so that the loss of any potentially pleasant or valuable life can be seen as possessing a negative value, as a reasonable object of avoidance. The element of negative valuation is made possible by the introduction of the notion of what the person could have been, could have done, or could have enjoyed, and so forth. Now we will try to understand further the logic of the superlimiting conception by posing the question: What sort of "could have" is represented in these expressions?

I advance and argue for the thesis that the notion of possibility expressed by *could have* in this context is that of subjunctive or counterfactual possibility. My thesis is that when we say of a person who has died that his death was tragic or evil or otherwise evaluate it negatively, we imply that if he had survived (contrary to fact) his hypothetical continued existence would have been self-satisfying or good or otherwise positively evaluated. I will call this the *counterlimit thesis* to indicate that it is based on the superlimiting view of death and is an essentially counterfactual thesis. It may help to state the counterlimit thesis symbolically, to display its components clearly. First, let us assume that death is a "state" that an individual can "enter into" at a time, t, and write this as $\ulcorner D_{a,t} \urcorner$. Further, we need to assume that a person may remain alive at a time t, that is, not die at t, $\ulcorner \neg D_{a,t} \urcorner$. Third, an individual may remain alive, or survive, or not be in a state of being dead, over an interval of time. If this interval commences at t, it may be written $\ulcorner t + \Delta \urcorner$ to signify some indefinite interval subsequent to and including t. Finally, we assume that the death or survival of an individual may be evaluated positively or negatively. Accordingly, we might represent "a's dying at t was negative" as $\ulcorner D_{a,t}^- \urcorner$, or "$a$'s survival during $t + \Delta$ was positive" as $\ulcorner \neg D_{a,t+\Delta}^+ \urcorner$. Now the *counterlimit thesis* is stated:

(CT1) $D_{a,t}^- \rightarrow (\neg D_{a,t} \;\square\!\!\rightarrow\; \neg D_{a,t+\Delta}^+)$

Or to paraphrase again: If a's death at t was negative, then it follows logically that if a had not died at t then his state of continued survival during $t + \Delta$ would have been positive. The $\rightarrow$ represents logical implication or what is sometimes called strict implication.[2] The $\square\!\!\rightarrow$ represents counterfactual implication. Read $\ulcorner p \;\square\!\!\rightarrow\; q \urcorner$ as "If p were the case then q would be the case." Now that we have barely stated the counterlimit thesis, we must provide an elucidation of how the terms in it are to be extactly taken, and distinguish some variants of it.

2. See Hughes and Cresswell (1968).

Counterfactuals

The characteristic feature of the counterlimiting thesis, that aspect of it that calls for the most commentary and analysis, is the $\square\!\!\rightarrow$ relation. By comparison, the relation of logical implication, $\rightarrow$, while perhaps equally controversial to logicians, requires little comment here, and little of direct or obvious significance turns on the preferred account of this symbol as far as our immediate interests are concerned. One comment is in order however. Some theoreticians of thanatology may wish to replace $\rightarrow$ with the symbol for logical equivalence, thus making the counterlimit thesis into an equation, an expression of the "if and only if" variety. As (CT1) stands, it offers only the assertion that the counterfactual "If he had lived, his life would have been valuable" as a necessary condition of "His death was tragic." But if we require also that the former be a sufficient condition of the tragedy, or negative value of death, then the thesis becomes an equivalence.

(CT2) $D_{a,t}^{-} \leftrightarrow (\neg D_{a,t} \;\square\!\!\rightarrow\; \neg D_{a,t+\Delta}^{+})$

Perhaps the counterlimit thesis can be strengthened in this way, and certainly (CT2) is an extension worth note, but I will confine my remarks in the sequel to the weaker thesis (CT1).

Now to turn to $\square\!\!\rightarrow$, the variably strict conditional. The account that follows is that of Lewis (1973). For each variably strict condition there must be an assignment to a world i of a set $\$i$ of spheres of accessibility around i. A sphere around a world i is to contain just those worlds that resemble i to a certain degree. The smaller the sphere, the more similar to i is the world that falls within it. Formal constraints on the definition of a centered system of spheres are given in Lewis (1973, pp. 14f.). A counterfactual $\ulcorner\varnothing \;\square\!\!\rightarrow\; \Psi\urcorner$ is true at a world i, according to a system of spheres $\$$, if and only if either (1) no world belongs to any sphere S in $\$i$, or (2) some sphere S in $\$i$ does contain at least one $\varnothing$-world, and $\varnothing \supset \Psi$ holds at every world in S (Lewis, 1973, p. 16). Roughly this amounts to the following. A counterfactual is vacuously true if there is no world sufficiently similar to the world of the antecedent. A counterfactual is non-vacuously true if the consequent is true in every world that is sufficiently similar to the world of the antecedent. What Lewis calls a "might-counterfactual" is non-vacuously true if the consequent is true in some world that is sufficiently similar to the world of the antecedent. The might-counterfactual can be defined in terms of the would-counterfactual as follows.

$$\varnothing \diamondsuit\!\!\rightarrow \Psi =_{df} \neg(\varnothing \ \square\!\!\rightarrow \neg\Psi)$$

The difference between the "might" and "would" counterfactuals are exemplified in the contrast between "If I survived, I would have a pleasant life" and "If I survived, I might have a pleasant life." Thus yet a weaker, but still interesting, variant of the counterlimit thesis can be stated.

(CTo) $D^-_{a,t} \rightarrow (\neg D_{a,t} \diamondsuit\!\!\rightarrow \neg D^+_{a,t+\Delta})$

According to this version, it is only required for my death to be negatively valued that if I were to survive, my continuing life might have a positive value. In other words, (CTo) makes it even easier to argue that a death is tragic or evil than (CT1). Although (CT1) is a more central thesis for our purposes here in some ways, (CTo) is also an interesting variant for thanatology to consider.

Although we have used Lewis's treatment of counterfactuals in the analysis of (CT1) and its variants, the possible world semantics of Stalnaker (1968) could also be applicable. This account rules that a counterfactual "If $\varnothing$ were true then Ψ would be true" is true in a given world, say the actual world ζ, if and only if Ψ is true in the possible world β that is the most similar world to ζ. Stalnaker's analysis turns on the assumption that there is a unique possible world, β, that is more like the actual world than any other possible world. Lewis (1973) argues, on the contrary, that there may be no such world that is maximally similar to a given world. That is, perhaps for every world that is similar to a given world, there is always a world that is more similar. Thus possible worlds could get more and more similar to the actual world without limit. So instead of demanding maximal similarity, Lewis requires only comparative similarity of worlds to underwrite a counterfactual. According to Lewis, "If $\varnothing$ were true then Ψ would be true" is true in a given world, say the actual world ζ, if and only if there is a world β in which $\ulcorner\varnothing \ \& \ \Psi\urcorner$ is true that is more like ζ than any other world γ in which $\ulcorner\varnothing \ \& \ \neg\Psi\urcorner$ is true. A variant of Stalnaker's account due to Pollock (1976) and a treatment of Åqvist (1973) not dissimilar to Lewis's could also be applicable to superlimiting thanatological contexts, but we do not pursue these matters here. Further research will possibly bring out the finer shades of counterfactual discriminations implicit in (CT1), utilizing these various counterfactual logics.

Counterparts

A problem for superlimiting thanatologic glimpsed in the previous chapter is posed by the observation that the person "Jones," whose name occurs in the sentences "Jones died in 1958" and "Jones' death was tragic," does not exist at the time of the writing of these sentences. The problem could be phrased this way: what do referring expressions refer to in sentences about the dead? They certainly don't refer to actual, that is, living persons, on the secular hypothesis at any rate. To put it yet another way, if I kill you, who is the victim of the crime, who is the subject of my wrongdoing, the person whose death was caused by me? I can hardly be said to be guilty of murder if the victim still exists as a person, but I can scarcely be guilty likewise if the object of my act has ceased to exist altogether. A coherent claim of victimhood demands some object of reference that is the victim, the subject, or object, of the crime.

The limiting conception of death deals with the problem by ruling that we have no direct knowledge of death and therefore that any postulated form of continued existence is simply an unknowable *arcanum*, beyond experience and therefore beyond the realm of meaningful discourse. Van Evra (1971) writes that the view of death as limit removes the need to talk of experienceless selves and similar obscure entities. However, we have already intimated that this application of Occam's razor makes it problematic to underwrite the notion that death is an evil, a negative value, or tragic, that the person who is reduced to the state of a contented infant by a brain injury has suffered a misfortune. Thus on the superlimiting, secular view of death, some means of coping with these contexts of thanatological discourse are required.

I propose the following solution. When we say of Jones, who died in 1958, that his death was tragic because of what he could have done, or could have been in 1959 or 1960, we refer not to the existent Jones in the actual world, but to a counterpart of Jones in a possible world. The proposal is that our problem admits of treatment by the counterpart theory of Lewis (1968 and 1971), a component of Lewis's possible worlds semantics for counterfactuals. We refer the reader to these two articles and Lewis's remarks on counterparts in his 1973 work for a detailed formal account of this notion, but we include here a brief introduction to the intuitive idea involved, for readers not familiar with it.

A main problem in understanding *possibilia*, unactualized possibles, entities not in the actual world, is the apparent lack of criteria of identity for them. Within a given possible world, much the same notion of identity can be carried over from the one we utilize in making judgements of identity between objects in the actual world (however this notion is to be analyzed), but the problem becomes especially acute when we need to say that an object in one world (say the actual world) is identical to an object in some possible world that is accessible to the former world. This is often called the problem of "trans-world identity." Lewis meets the problem by ruling that things in different worlds are never identical—rather that an object in world ζ may have a *counterpart* in world β, an object that resembles it, but is not strictly identical to it. Thus, according to Lewis's theory, you exist in the actual world only, but you have counterparts in various possible worlds. Your counterparts in these possible worlds resemble you (in the actual world) more closely than do the other things in these worlds, but they are not identical to you. To put it as Lewis (1968, p. 115) does, your counterparts are the persons you would have been, had the world been otherwise.

Counterpart theory provides the semantical foundations for the superlimiting conception of death as follows. If we truly assert that Jones died in 1958 and that his death was tragic, then it follows by (CT1) that if Jones had survived, his continued life would have had a positive value. Translated out into the language of counterparts, the latter requirement reads: there is a possible world β, that diverged from the actual world, ζ, at some time in 1958, that is accessible to ζ, and where some counterpart of Jones-in-ζ continued to live a valuable life. Insofar as we can attach a positive value to the continued survival of the counterpart of Jones in β, we can justify attaching a negative value to the actual death of Jones in ζ. Thus superlimiting valuations are vindicated.

Unactualized Possibles

The discussion under Counterfactual and Counterparts may seem to some readers to be, if not verging on the assumption of some suspect form of *post mortem* survival of the individual who has died, at least violating philosophical economy by populating the world with possible persons. Clearly much turns on how much of this sort of talk is allowed and how we are to think of unactualized possibles. Following Rescher (1973), we suggest that possible persons are best thought of as hypothetical possibilities that do not exist as such, but must be imagined, or assumed, or postulated in such a way that they are essentially mind-dependent. It is well to be clear that only actual things or persons can be said to exist in the actual world. Unactualized possibles can, in a sense, be said to "exist" or "subsist" (to use a term once suggested by Russell) but not "unqualifiedly in themselves, but in a relativized manner, as the objects of certain intellectual processes" (Rescher, 1973, p. 215). Thus their existence is clearly mind-dependent and not to be confused with actual existence independent of a conceiving mind.

On the other hand, the individuals that inhabit possible worlds are not mind-dependent in the sense that they are purely psychological entities, dependent on this or that particular conceiver. It is more accurate to say that the general concept of a possible person is essentially mind-dependent in the sense that the meaning of the very notion involves some mind-dependent operation such as conceiving, imagining, conjecturing, and so forth. Possible persons are not subjective in the sense that we cannot make true statements about them that can be objectively confirmed, but they are subjective in the limited sense that they are conceptual objects only and not to be confused with actual objects. As Rescher puts it, their *esse* is *concipi* (to be conceived), unlike sensible objects, of which Berkeley is said to have written, *esse est percipi*.[3]

The counterparts of persons in possible worlds are not to be thought of as actual survivors or living persons, even ghostly or spiritual ones, any more than a possible world is to be equated with

3. Although many people attribute the phrase *esse est percipi* to Berkeley, George Hughes tells me that he has never found it in Berkeley, never seen a reference for it, and strongly suspects that he never wrote it. Berkeley does however, say, of sensible objects, that their *esse* is *percipi*.

the actual world. There is all the difference here between what could exist but might not, and what does actually exist. Thus counterpart theory, as we interpret it, can allow the secular conception of the total and irreversible extinction of actual survival of the individual as an experiencing subject in death. At least there need be no inconsistency between the secular and superlimiting concepts. Of course, for those who do not accept the mind-dependency of unactualized possibles, the problem of reconciling these two approaches is likely to remain a source of considerable difficulty.

A main objection to superlimiting conceptions of death generally is that in requiring reference to possible individuals they may seem to require the postulation of a "ghostly entity" that survives death, thus apparently contravening the secular view of death. To support the superlimiting view, it has seemed that the self must continue to exist, and the limiting theorist is quick to point out how such obscure and metaphysical assumptions lead to paradox, and perhaps even to some form of spiritualism. But counterpart theory ameliorates the difficulty for the superlimiting theorist because it eliminates any need to require that actual entities exist in any other world than the actual world. Therefore the idiom of actual survival of an existent individual need be apposite only to the actual world. Possible persons need not be actual persons, much less actual ghosts or spirits (or even possible ghosts or spirits). Thus counterpart theory assures the secular conception of the consistency of its assumption of the total and irreversible extinction of consciousness and personal survival of death. A counterpart does not "survive," nor need it even exist (in the actual world). Possible worlds and the counterparts that occur in them may be "mere scenarios," worlds that could possibly have been actualized, and nothing more.

Of course the method of counterparts is not the only way to support the modal idiom of (CT1), but it is representative of the methods of modal logic that can be used for this purpose. Counterpart theory is by no means problem-free either, but at its state of development by Lewis, it offers a promising means of providing an important segment of the foundational logical structure of the superlimiting conception, and provides an initial defence against some of the cruder objections to the superlimiting idiom. I do not wish to imply that counterpart logic solves all the problems of the superlimiting view—quite the contrary, it really opens up a variety of more sophisticated linguistic difficulties—yet the *dubia* become less dubious by its introduction. To be sure however, the limiting view remains the safer view of the two, committed to less proliferation of potentially troublesome abstract entities.

Death as Experience and Projection

We now return to a discussion of the adequacy conditions set out in chapter IV in the light of subsequent developments. There we thought of death in various ways within the framework of the analogy of a point on a line, wondering whether death is best thought of as the rightmost segment including the point, or excluding the point, or just the point itself, or a stretch along the line, or the pair of segments (possibly including or excluding the point), and so forth. We will adopt the eclectic strategy of combining the limiting and superlimiting approaches into a unified conception by suggesting a bipartite view of death as experience and projection. First, the view of death as limit captures death from the first-person point of view of the experiencing subject. For him, death is a limit that he moves towards but that always remains outside the field of experience. This field represents the left segment of the line, approaching but not including the point that divides it from the right side.

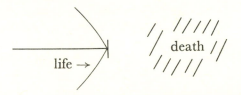

The point and right segment represent a domain that is, on the secular conception, beyond experience, but the living person can make inferences beyond this domain. But how can he make conjectures about a person that, at that time, will be dead and hence not actually exist? Or how can the now-living make true statements at all about the now-dead if the latter do not exist? What can they be talking about? The subjects of this discourse are, as we have seen, mind-dependent projections extrapolated from experience that allow us to talk about what could happen. Counterparts or possible persons are to possible worlds as actual persons are to the actual world. But according to the secular view, there is a very strict distinction between the two domains—one is the domain of life, consciousness, and experience, the actual world; the other is simply a projection from the former, but one that is emphatically beyond experience in a very important sense.

This binary view should now help to explain the sense in which death is thought to be a null state. It is empty of experience, of consciousness, of first-person actuality, but it is a state insofar as it is a projection of the mind beyond experience, but based on experience. We can see how it is reasonable that we should think of death as occuring instantaneously. Since death is beyond experience, it is not within the actual time-flow of the individual's experience, it is merely a point that we postulate in a possible world, and therefore it is unexceptionable that it should be thought of as infinitesimal. Likewise that death is a mind-dependent projection resolves our earlier problems about its infinite duration. Finally, the dual view of death is compatible with the notion that death comes after life insofar as we are thinking of a future-directed projection.

The dual view does, however, contain a paradox analogous to Zeno's paradoxes. The actual person moves towards death but never actually reaches death—death, the limit, is unattainable. It is merely a possible person who is dead. Thus it seems to follow that actual persons never die. This consequence may be seen to be a fallacy however, as we can recognize by remembering the distinction between dying and death. Actual persons can, without paradox, experience the process of dying. But of course they cannot reach the point of death, since, by hypothesis, at this point they have ceased to be actual. Yet it does seem to be a legitimate consequence of the two-part view of death that actual persons are not dead. And this is bound to seem paradoxical. In defense of this consequence, we should add that denial of it might be thought to be even more paradoxical for the secular theorist, who does not wish to postulate actual survivors.

Further sting can be removed from this apparent paradox, and some of our earlier difficulties of chapter IV resolved as well, if we bring into consideration the viewpoint of the other, as well as the viewpoint of the *moriturus* himself. So far we have looked at death in the dual theory exclusively as a projection of one person towards his own death. In so doing, we have naturally favored the idea that death is an instantaneous transformation and neglected the suggestion of chapter IV that death is often thought of as an event that takes place over an interval. Now, to complement the dual view, a view admittedly biased in favor of the experiencing subject's consciousness of his own death, we suggest that if the death of another is the notion we wish to capture, the framework of death as event is most natural. In other words, if I am thinking of my own death, the dual view is the suggested philosophical reconstruction of what is taking place. But if I am thinking of the death of Socrates, an altogether different model may be appropriate. Here I seem to be thinking more of an event or even a gradual process—Socrates discoursing with his students, swallowing the hemlock, his feet becoming numb, and so forth. Admittedly, the view of death as event, has its complications, as we saw in chapter IV. Presumably, events are not permanent, unlike death, so more than simply an event must be involved, or at least an ordinary event. But I will not dwell on the further analysis of death as event here, being primarily concerned to elaborate the dual view as a first person point of view of death.

Yet a further refinement is necessary. According to the view of death as limit, it is not quite accurate to say that death is a point or state-change rather than an event or interval because that very point, following Wittgenstein, is not within the field of consciousness of the *moriturus*. Consequently, it seems to me that we are required to adopt the following thesis. From the point of view of the individual involved, there is no distinction between the event death and the state-change death. As he projects beyond the limit, there is no experiential basis for drawing any distinction between an instantaneous point or an extended interval. Even if he could contemplate such a distinction, it does not seem important to do so in the dual framework. But from the point of view of an observer there is a significant difference between event and state-change. Here death may be seen either as a gradual process like birth or as an instantaneous state-change. What is a deep ambivalence in the observer's framework of death seems trivial and inappropriate from the point of view of one's own death.

Readers who strongly prefer the notion of death as an event might well be expected to complain that the dual approach does not do justice to the underlying physical reality of death the event, that the dual view is too subjectively or epistemically oriented. This may be a legitimate criticism, or the basis of one, but an advantage of the dual approach is that it does explain the epistemic features of chapter IV surprisingly well. It does explain how knowledge of death based on experience is possible, while at the same time showing how knowledge of death is intrinsically limited by lack of first-person data,[4] and thus lays the foundations for a Kantian critique of death. With its emphasis on consciousness, experience, and mind-based projections, it is an admittedly mind-oriented approach. Yet, insofar as mental states can be correlated with brain-states, an underlying physical basis of the dual view is ready at hand. Death is characterized by the irreversible cessation of experience and consciousness in the individual, and criteria best adapted to estimating the time of onset of irreversible coma are most likely to be associated with EEG measurements, angiography, or other indications of cerebration rather than with non-cerebral-based criteria. In short, the dual concept of death has an affinity with brain death. Yet even if the dual view is not the final word on all aspects of death, brain death is important enough a concept to make its affinity with the dual view enhance, rather than detract from, the latter. Fletcher (1973, p. 100) writes that the cardinal indicator of human personhood is the neocortical function: " . . . to be dead 'humanly' speaking is to be ex-cerebral, no matter how long the *body* remains alive." But why is brain death commonly thought to be so important? The basis for an answer is to be found in the centrality of the dual view, with its emphasis on experience and consciousness.

This point is particularly clearly made by Van Till (1975, p. 136) where it is argued that the criterion for declaration of death must not be decided on the basis of value judgement, but on the objective basis of whether or not a person has certain faculties. "Ethically the faculty to perceive, which enables a person to take part in interhuman communication and to feel pain, is the critical element in determining if a living human organism is to be considered and treated as a living person. The quantitative question of how well perception functions is not relevant for the diagnosis of death; the sole criterion should be whether there is perception at all." For Van Till, the physiological factor of critical importance is the functioning

4. Łukasiewicz in "On the History of the Logic of Propositions" (*Polish Logic, 1920–1939*, ed. Storrs McCall, Oxford: The Clarendon Press, 1967, p. 75) mentions an ancient syllogism quoted by Origen in *Contra Celsium*: "If *p* then *q*; if *p* then not-*q*; therefore not-*p*." The example given is a fascinating specimen of Stoic logic: "If you know that you are dead, then you are dead (for nothing false can be known); if you know that you are dead then you are not dead (for the dead know nothing); therefore you do not know that you are dead."

of synapses and neurones in the brain, but what she calls the philosophical criterion is the total and permanent disintegration of the psychosomatic entity. In her view, philosophical death occurs when and only when physiological death (brain death) occurs (Van Till, 1975, p. 137).

That death is to be equated philosophically with the permanent absence of perception is very much in accord with the dual view of death, and in our opinion confirms the centrality of the dual view of death. The dual view explains how the notion of perception is at the basis of the logic of death. Moreover, we can now see clearly how the dual view can function as a logic of death, a philosophical foundation against which proposed physiological and other kinds of measurements and criteria concerning death can be partially evaluated. There are many ways to evaluate the concept of brain death as being a concept of death that is ethically, or medically, central, or significant in any number of ways. But insofar as brain death may be equated with the dual view (and this equation is highly plausible to say the least), the philosophical centrality of brain death is made apparent.

The point is also made by Kass (1971) that the redefiners of death are not solely concerned with utilitarian, ethical, sociological, legal, or donor-eligibility factors—they operate on the presumption that there is an underlying fact of death and that their criteria are "true criteria." We assume that medicine and science are capable of determining death, and we also assume that there is a concept "death" that they set out to determine, that criteria for determination can be evaluated against this concept, and that some criteria are more true of it than others. I propose that the dual view, possibly supplemented by a notion of death as event, adequately represents a central traditional concept of death and that diagnostic criteria for determining death are only true, or correspond to the fact of death, insofar as they approach the target marked out by the dual theory of death. I would add the obvious suggestion that the kind of criteria proposed for brain death have more affinity with the dual view than do respiratory, circulatory (extra-cerebral), cellular, or other kinds of criteria.

Concluding Remarks

We have raised, and, we hope, clearly expressed, a number of related analytical, methodological questions pertaining to the concept of death. More constructively, we have attempted to lay the logical foundations for a theory that has at least the capability to answer some of these questions and provide a basis in theory for answering others. Much remains to be done and it is quite clear that the theory is by no means in a refined state of development, but it is my contention that the theory is (a) reasonably adequate to a standard, central, and traditional notion of death; (b) applicable to bio-medical, legal, ethical, and psychological problems; (c) clear and intuitively forceful; (d) free at least of the obvious inconsistencies and paradoxes; (e) fruitful, because stated in terms familiar in philosophical logic; and (f) relatively simple and economical. I expect that a major block to acceptability for some may be the notion of unactualized possible individuals, but for these readers the limiting part of the theory may be of use even though the super-limiting part provides difficulties. Nevertheless, I have tried to defend the necessity of the superlimiting conception.

It is of course a truism that "mere semantics" will not solve the substantive problems of death and euthanasia, but it would be quite fallacious to infer that philosophical abstractions have no role at all to play in understanding death. The variety of medical redefinitions prompts a skeptic like Morison (1971) to argue that there is no "magic moment" of death at all, simply a gradual and piecemeal dying of various organs, that death is merely a literary personification of the dying moments, a traditional myth of no scientific import. On the contrary, death is very real, if anything is, and a traditional secular notion of death is describable in scientifically and logically well-written language. Certainly the bulk of our concern with death should be empirical and practical, even emotional and compassionate, but there is a place for being logical and trying to think clearly about death too, as the example of Socrates should remind us.

The movement of our argument throughout this study so far has been in the direction of attempting to resist the apparent pluralism of the heterogeneous diagnostic criteria of chapter III by trying to formulate a unified concept of death at the conceptual or philo-sophical level, against which these criteria may be arrayed and ordered. But, one may well ask—is such a resistance desirable or even necessary? If advances in medical technology strongly suggest a pluralistic view of death, resisting it is surely dogmatic and un-progressive. Certainly I would have to agree that if it could be shown that advances at the more pratical levels of criteria and diagnostic procedures demanded, required, or even led on the basis of strong arguments to an irreducibly pluralistic philosophy of death, we should not resist such a force. Indeed, I have been at pains throughout to argue that any adequate view of death must be not only theoretically adequate, but also practically adequate in the sense of being commensurate with data and criteria of the medical practice of death and dying. But also I strongly feel that in dealing with the analysis of death, the needs of practice must be balanced against the constraints of theory. Letting technology lead us by the nose, so to speak, is a basic error, as bad an error as indulging in empty philosophical theorizing. The concept of death is both an ethical and social notion, containing valuative elements and replete with significant social and broad philosophical issues. So the technology of criteria must be weighed against other considerations. In other words, I do not wish to argue that a pluralistic conception of death as such must be incorrect. The literature on the philosophical analysis of death is in much too primitive a state to hazard any such strong hypothesis as that. I merely caution that a too-easy pluralism should not be uncritically acquiesced in.

We could put it this way. So far, I have not seen a strong argument for irreducible pluralism, although suggestions of such a pluralism are certainly numerous and worrisome. My work here is preliminary to this strong type of argument, whenever it is formulated, as it surely will be. I hope to have provided a general background against which future arguments of this type may be better evaluated. In the absence of pluralistic argument I also, of course, have attempted to provide some reasons for believing that the groundwork for a unified view of death can be laid out.

"How unified is the dual view?" one may well retort. After all, it is "dual," and moreover, as we noted, it also needs supplementation in the area of events. Does not this suggest that it is really a multiple view? Worse yet, it is a rather special view of death as a lack of experience, even labelled a "secular" view. Does this not require even further supplementation, diversity, and complexity? All these insinuations are of course quite accurate in their suggestion that the dual view is widely ramified, replete with unsolved difficulties of analysis, and evidently in need of considerable supplementation and elaboration of one kind and another. Theories are like that. I would make only the comparatively modest claim, however, that the dual view at least shows us one, I think rather attractive, way out of an apparently stultifying concretism of remaining exclusively at the practical levels of chapter II. The dual approach gives some promise of the moderating and unifying influence of theory. But the really hard questions of pluralism are a thing of the future. And just how liberated a pluralism the dual theory may turn out to tolerate can only be evaluated through further research, stimulated, I hope, by this discussion.

Chapter VI

The Religious Conception of Death

The directly relevant literature on the secular theory of death we proposed is extremely slim, and consequently most of what we have had to say is for the most part relatively new. The literature on religious views of death is, however, enormous,[1] and therefore we are restricted to attempting to summarize the main ideas and commenting on what seem to be the most important logical and philosophical aspects of these basic ideas. It is not possible to do justice to religious tradition in a short chapter, but some philosophical remarks on the key notions may prove an instructive counterbalance to the secular views with which we have been mainly preoccupied. Indeed, it is not because of a bias in favor of the secular view that we concentrate on it, but rather it is because the secular view, due to its relative lack of previous attempts at clear articulation, is in greater need of formulation if anything near parity of philosophical expression is to be attained between the two views. On the other hand, while there have been many more attempts to systematize the Christian view of death,[2] the literature also exhibits considerable disagreement and difference among interpretations. Somewhat arbitrarily, we will confine ourselves mainly to the Christian religious view of death.

Two Views of Immortality

There seems to be a widespread popular confusion between the Greek view of the immortality of the soul and the (New Testament) Christian view of the resurrection of the body.[3] It seems that later

1. For fuller treatments, the reader might look to Lewis (1973) and Dixon (1975). Here and in note 14, the reference is to Hywel D. Lewis, 1973. All other references to Lewis (1973) are to David Lewis, 1973.
2. This theme is developed in the readings in Flew (1964) and bibliography.
3. Cullman (1958) and Choron (1963) provide accounts of the historical basis of this distinction. Jaeger (1947) is also helpful in this respect.

Christianity has effected a link between the two views to the extent that nowadays they are commonly elided together by Christians. However, in the early Christian teachings, the doctrine of immortality is clearly and emphatically distinct from the Greek view found, for example, in Plato. In Plato there is a dualism between mind (or soul) and body that has continued, through Descartes, to exert a strong influence on western thought. In various of the dialogues the hypothesis is entertained that the soul does not perish with the dissolution of the body, but survives in some disembodied form. Plato is never dogmatic about this hypothesis, and considers various arguments for and against its plausibility, treating the subject in a rational and philosophic spirit. In the *Phaedo*, some arguments for the immortality of the soul are advanced—a brief account of these conveys the flavor of the Platonic treatment: (1) The hypothesis that the soul existed before birth is a corollary of the theory that all genuine knowledge is recollection. (The Platonic theory of learning is based on recollection.) Thus it is possible that the soul likewise exists after death. (2) The soul is capable of knowing the Forms or Ideas (general concepts); these are non-spatio-temporal. Therefore the soul itself must be outside time and space and consequently indestructible and immortal. (3) The soul rules the body, and therein resembles the immortal gods. (4) The soul is simple, and therefore incapable of dissolution. (5) The essence of the soul is life, the opposite of death. Therefore the soul cannot be conceived of as dying, any more than fire can be conceived of as becoming cold. (6) The soul is self-moved, the source of motion, and therefore can never cease to move. Plato was aware of the inadequacy of these arguments however, and left open the possibility that death could be either dreamless sleep, or the migration of the soul to another world.[4]

In modern philosophy, the Greek conception of immortality has made its influence felt in the philosophy of Descartes, with its dualistic separation of mind and body. Descartes, in his *Passions of the Soul*, argued that the soul can absent itself from the body at death: since all dead bodies are devoid of heat, some infer that it is the absence of the soul that has caused the heat and movement to cease. On the contrary, the reason why the soul *absents itself* is that the heat ceases and the organs disintegrate (Article 5). Thus the soul is independent of the body—death comes not because the soul dis-

4. See also the account of Choron (1958).

integrates, but because the principal parts of the body disintegrate. The body is like a machine, and a dead body is simply like a broken machine in which the movement ceases to act, like a watch when the spring is broken. When the bodily organs disintegrate, the soul withdraws from the body. The soul does not disintegrate, because it is not even spatial. These doctrines, based on the notion of an immaterial non-spatial soul, independent of the body, are very much a continuation of the Greek view.[5]

The doctrine of St. Paul, found in the New Testament, is one of the resurrection of the body, and is therefore fundamentally distinct from the Greek hypothesis of the survival of a disembodied soul. According to the Christian doctrine, there will be a resurrection of the dead on the Last Day of Judgement. The graves will be opened, and saint and sinner will stand before the Son of God and be judged. St. Paul distinguishes between the natural (sarkical) man and the spiritual (pneumatic) man. It is the latter who received the Spirit of God, and who is the recipient of the divine spark. The pneumatic man arises through the natural man through conversion, a kind of rebirth. This rebirth is a gift of God, and cannot be obtained by simple desire alone.[6] The pneumatic man is both flesh and spirit— he has an outward and an inward aspect. In Plato, the soul is pure and the body is the source of evil, but in St. Paul, the whole natural man (body and soul) is sinful. The pneumatic man is a totality and includes the body also. Thus the resurrection of the body is not quite as simple or unsophisticated a notion as it may initially appear to be.

In the Greek view, death is something natural, but in the Christian view death is abnormal, unnatural, opposed to God: "death is the wages of sin." St. Augustine, in the *City of God* writes that the first men were punished with death because they were sinners. He refers of course to the doctrine of the fall of man from paradise.

According to the teachings of some churches, there is a temporal gap between death and resurrection—in this period the soul enters into a state of silence, inactivity, and unconsciousness immediately after death. On this hypothesis, it would seem that the soul is disembodied for a time, and therefore this view seems to incorporate elements of the Greek view. In Catholic teaching however, there is no temporal gap—the souls of the dead go immediately after death

5. Further details are given by Choron (1958) and Flew (1964, Introduction).
6. See Cullman (1958).

into heaven, purgatory, or hell.[7] Which state is reached depends first on a self-judgement, for or against God, by the individual concerned, and second on the judgement of Christ. A decision for Christ by the individual in the first place is however not possible without the help of Christ. Purgatory is thought to be a somewhat painful state in which the soul is freed from its inclination to sin preparatory to its movement into heaven. It is a kind of delayed entry of unpunished or unforgiven "venial sin" as opposed to more serious "mortal sin" that is the cause of eternal damnation.

Protestants deny the existence of purgatory, and most Protestants believe that the soul goes immediately after death to heaven or hell.

Price's Two Conceptions of the Next World

Taking up the theme of the two traditional conceptions of afterlife, the *embodied* and *disembodied* conceptions, Price (1971, ch. 6) attempts to go beyond the usual analogies and metaphors to reconstruct a consistent and philosophically adequate theory corresponding to each. According to the embodied conception, we have to think of a material world with spatial attributes, although the space of the Next World might not be Euclidean or three-dimensional. The Next World would have to have "secondary qualities" such as color, sound, and smell, and causal properties, such as weight, elasticity, and rigidity. Immediately a philosophical difficulty is apparent—where is this quasi-material Next World? According to Price, it is conceivable that there are many different spaces in our universe, or if there is only one space, that it has other than our three dimensions. To form an idea of the world of the disembodied conception, Price suggests that it could be a kind of dream-world: as in a dream, in death we are deprived of sensory stimuli, but we may nevertheless have very vivid and exciting imaginary experiences. Accordingly, life after death would be a kind of dream from which we would never wake up, in which we retain our memories, desires, and personalities. Then death would simply be a change of consciousness, something like what happens now when we fall asleep and begin to dream.

Dream images have spatial properties, but they are not located in physical space. Thus the dream world supplied by memory would

7. See Dixon (1975).

be much like the physical world, except that the causal laws would be different. For example, if a person desires to be in a certain place, he would immediately find himself in it, without any intermediate passage (Price, 1971, p. 107). Thus a person would usually be able to infer that, despite the familiar environment, he is no longer alive.

There is the frightening prospect, as noticed by Penelhum (1970, p. 51), of solipsism. Since the survivor cannot perceive anything, he could not perceive, or communicate with, other persons. Price responds by arguing that, although there would be many Next Worlds, telepathy within a given world should be taken into account, citing known instances of telepathic dreams and communications in psychical research. Even this is not really very satisfactory however, for in order to have social relations, a person must have a body. Price (1971, pp. 110f.) argues that in order to be a person, you must have, for example, a face, which others can recognize and respond to. You must have some means of expressing yourself in an overt and perceptible manner. But second, a person has to be recognizable to enter into social relations of a very significant kind. The post-mortem body might be quite different from the physical body, but it must resemble the physical body.

Thus Price concludes that personal survival requires some form of embodiment. To fulfill this without postulating an actual physical body, Price postulates an *image-body*, a public entity but not one located in physical space—public only to all those others with whom one has social relations. So, in effect, the two theories converge—in the disembodied conception there turns out to be some sort of body postulated. Thus Price concludes that the two theories are complementary, rather than opposed. The physical and psychological analogies we began with really both come around to something that is intermediate between the physical and mental.

Problems in the Religious View

The fact that, on the secular hypothesis, the dead cease to exist poses a problem of finding points of reference for statements about the dead, a problem met by the superlimiting theory. But there is no analogous difficulty for the religious hypothesis, which has it that the dead continue to exist as individuals, complete with personality and memory, thus providing obvious candidates for points of reference for statements about the dead. Thus presumably, the philosophical difficulties we posed for the secular conception are easily met on the religious view. On the former view, death is a transformation from actuality to mere possibility, or hypothetical existence, whereas on the religious view, death is transformation from earthly actual existence to some other form of actual existence—instead of cessation, there is simply a continuity, although the form of existence is presumably modified. It is a question of more of the same. Somewhat unexpectedly, from a point of view of conceptual structure, the secular view is the more difficult one to reconstruct. I would even go so far as to suggest that a philosopher of religious inclination might see this as an argument against the plausibility of the secular hypothesis—it is so plagued with paradox that it is hard enough to understand what it says, let alone give assent to it. However, in my view, the dual theory of death adequately deals with the secular paradoxes and dubia. The religious conception is not, however, entirely free of difficulties of its own. Skeptics like Flew (1955) have raised the objection that the religious hypothesis is unverifiable, and others, for example, Penelhum (1970) and Clarke (1971), have questioned whether and how survivors in the Next World may be said to be *identical* with their historical counterparts. Certainly there is an enormous literature on these kinds of issues. I might comment however that defenders of forms of the religious conception like Hick (1957) and Price (1972) have reconstructed the religious conception in scenarios that seem at least consistent and philosophically respectable. The difficulty for the skeptic rather resides in the question of justification: what reason do we have to believe that these *prima facie* implausible conjectures might be true?[8]

Hick on Resurrection

The doctrine of eschatological verification proposed by John Hick (1957 and 1968) constitute a response to the challenge of Flew (1955) that religious utterances are cognitively meaningless. To meet the challenge, it is not required to establish that the Christian concept of an afterlife is verifiable in the sense that it is actually known to be

8. The reader is referred to Lamont (1952) for a fuller statement of these issues. Similar objections are discussed by Phillips (1970) and Flew (1964). Also very useful in this connection is the work of Ducasse (1961).

true, but only verifiable in the sense that it is possible to know that it is true, i.e., the hypothesis must be logically consistent and we must know what sorts of experience might constitute confirmation or disconformation of it. The hypothesis of the resurrection of the body, according to Hick, is verifiable but not falsifiable: if it is false then presumably nobody will ever know that it is false (unless some other hypothesis of survival is true), but if it is true, it is to be presumed that some of us will come to know that it is true.

To show that the Pauline hypothesis is consistent, Hick presents three pictures, each one of which, he claims is conceivable (if rather odd) and thus represents a consistent state of affairs. First, suppose a speaker at a learned gathering in England were to suddenly and inexplicably disappear, and suddenly reappear at some comparable meeting in Australia. The two persons are similar as to bodily and mental characteristics, memory, fingerprints, and so forth. A colleague flies to Australia to interview the missing professor, and he is unable to explain how, upon blinking his eyes, he simply found himself in a different room. Hick argues that, in this unusual case, we would extend our use of "same person" and call the itinerant professor the same person as the man who disappeared in England. Second picture: suppose the event is a death, only a replica of the individual, exactly as he was a moment before his death, appears in Australia. Even with the corpse on our hands, Hick still argues that we would say it was the same person who died and was miraculously recreated in Australia. Once again, the situation is bizarre, but not *logically* impossible. If the deceased person's colleagues were to interview him, presumably they would eventually begin treating him as the same person. Third picture: suppose that the replica appears not in Australia, but in a resurrection world inhabited by resurrected persons. The resurrected person remembers dying, and meets a number of relatives, historical personages, etc. There would presumably be no doubts about the identity of these various persons. The resurrection space might not be like physical space, or in our space, but there will be sufficient correspondence of characteristics and continuity of memory for us to speak of the *same persons* being in a new environment. This hypothesis may seem odd or unlikely, but it is far from apparent that it is logically impossible. Indeed, it does not take too much effort to imagine what such a state of affairs would be like, given the first two pictures. Thus Hick quite plausibly argues that one can conceive of afterlife experiences that would serve to verify the Pauline hypothesis. Of course mere survival would not verify theism, but Hick suggests two possible additional developments that would—an experience of the fulfillment of God's purpose for ourselves, and an experience of communion with God in the person of Christ.

Hick's argument that the Pauline conception of immortality he outlines is indeed a consistent hypothesis of a sort seems to be highly reasonable and convincing, and does thereby constitute, I feel, an effective rejoinder to Flew's challenge. Yet even granting this, the atheist or secular skeptic typically has the feeling that he has been sophistically refuted by Hick, and accordingly is not generally impressed by the notion of eschatological verification. More specifically, the secular respondent, at least in my experience, is bothered by two things: (1) the Pauline hypothesis does not seem initially very plausible; and (2) in this life we cannot know whether it is true, i.e., actual verification admittedly presupposes the truth of the hypothesis, that consequently seems to have the property of pulling itself up by its own bootstrings. The atheist senses a kind of dilemma: if evidence in this life counts towards the hypothesis, the preponderance of evidence seems to be against the hypothesis; if not, then the hypothesis is uninteresting since, by the lights of the atheist, this life is the only one that is or counts.

I feel that this reaction on the part of the secular thinker is extremely interesting, and that it genuinely reflects an underlying ambivalence in the logic of Hick's program. To reveal this ambivalence, I will, in the sequel, attempt to construct a counterargument to Hick's reasoning in the form of a dilemma that, I believe, uncovers the essential basis of the atheist's unease. The first step in the argument will be to distinguish generally between two kinds of verification.

Two Kinds of Verification

Despite the unresolved difficulties of studies in the logic of confirmation,[9] the inconclusive ongoing debate on the viability of an analytic-synthetic distinction,[10] and the overwhelming logical complexities

9. A detailed treatment is to be found in Hempel (1966, ch. 4) and Scheffler (1963).
10. See Hall (1966).

(some would say impossibility) of stating an adequate explication of the classical "verification principle,"[11] I would like to suggest that it is roughly accurate and reasonable to propose that there are, broadly speaking, two main types of "verification."

(V1)   A hypothesis, h, is (conclusively) verified only if h deductively implies at least one observation-sentence, p.

(V2)   A hypothesis, h, is (probabilistically) confirmed only if h inductively implies at least one observation-sentence, p.

Controversy on how to explicate the terms on the right side of (V1) and (V2) continues. Moreover, proponents of (V1) as the paradigm of verification have long argued that (V2) is peripheral or secondary. Conversely, other authors have argued that scientific explanation and verification are irreducibly stochastic, and that (V1) and its variants are relics of Newtonian science and not accurate models of most present-day scientific explanations.[12] However these philosophical controversies may ultimately be resolved, it is fair to say that both kinds of verification are *prima facie* plausible and are familiar enough in the literature that any general discussion of the topic must take both aspects provisionally into account. It seems quite reasonable to conjecture that both varieties of verification may have a legitimate role in the logic of the confirmation of hypotheses. because deductive logic is more firmly founded than the still highly controversial area of inductive logic, (V1) is often accorded more attention in discussions on the logic of confirmation, even though many, or perhaps even most interesting scientific hypotheses admit only of inductive verification through (V2).

The literature shows that it would be erroneous to think of (V1) and (V2) as providing definitions of two kinds of verification. Rather, what is indicated is that various qualifications on these two statements, concerning the use of analytical hypotheses and so forth, are required if (V1) and (V2) are to approach adequate explications of the concept of verification. Thus (V1) and (V2) are best regarded, for the present, as articles of scientific faith. Also (V1) and V2) do not rule on the question of the actual verification of a hypothesis, but on what is sometimes called "verifiability-in-principle." That is, (V1) and (V2) concern the question of whether a sequence constitutes a

11. See Hempel (1965).
12. See Rescher (1970).

well-formed hypothesis or whether it is merely a pseudo-hypothesis, a non-syntactically, well-formed expression. A hypothesis that is actually verified will be required to imply an observation-sentence that is true, or known to be true. But (V1) and (V2) are simply neutral in this respect. With these qualifications (V1) and (V2) allow us provisionally to distinguish between two broad kinds of verification.

A Dilemma

The question that produces the dilemma is: does Hick mean to cleave to (V1) exclusively, or can he allow (V2) also as a kind of verification that comes under the category of eschatological verification? First, let us assume that Hick does not include (V2), ruling accordingly that only first-hand, direct verification through experience can tend to confirm or disconfirm a hypothesis without any appeal at all to induction or probability.

The assumption that (V2) is thus excluded rules out, especially for the secular person, any possibility that there is any relevant evidence available in this life that bears at all on the hypothesis of immortality, provided that is is not possible for a person who is alive to have a direct first-hand experience of being dead. And this latter is a highly plausible assumption. Certainly we must say that it is extremely dubious that a person who is alive could experience being dead, for in order to truly experience being dead, he would presumably have to be dead, and then, by definition, he could not be "alive" at that time or ensuing times. Only the dead can experience being dead. On the secular hypothesis that death is accompanied by irreversible annihilation of all conscious experience, nobody ever experiences being dead (or even experiences death)[13]at all. On this

13. Indeed, to one who accepts the secular hypothesis, the notion of experiencing being dead is not only problematic but likely to be found incoherent. From this perspective, any juxtaposition of "experience" and "dead" may strongly seem paradoxical or inconsistent. In terms of the secular hypothesis, my statement "Only the dead can experience being dead" probably makes poetic sense at best. Even from the religious perspective, it is hard to avoid inconsistency in interpreting this statement and ones like it. One wants to say that anyone who experiences something is not really "dead," but at the same time it seems reasonable to infer that anyone who dies is dead. However, on the religious hypothesis, persons die but subsequently continue to experience something. It follows that such a person is both "dead" and "not dead" at the same

view, quite clearly, ruling out (V2) rules out any possibility that there can be any verification of the hypothesis of immortality. But this outcome is highly unsatisfactory for the secular skeptic, because it virtually rules out the possibility of verification or falsification of the hypothesis of immortality altogether. It is all very well for the Christian to reply "Wait and see" but this is hardly satisfying to the skeptic, and leaves him cut adrift from the possibility of evaluating the belief in immortality in light of the only kind of evidence that seems to him to be available, namely the experiences that we do have in this life. The religious person may make appeals to the authority of the scriptures, to the person of Christ, and so forth, but if he is consistent in excluding (V2) it is not altogether clear at all that these appeals are not specious. These kinds of appeals are not through first-hand direct experience, and do not appear to be conclusive in the sense required by (V1).

In rejecting (V2) the arguer for immortality leaves the skeptic bereft of any basis for evaluating his argument. Thus, to the secular person, the eschatological verificationist seems to be pulling himself up by his bootstraps. He says in effect: no evidence in this life can bear at all on my hypothesis of immortality. But this is quite clearly an outrage to anyone not already committed to the hypothesis, even if it is a delight to the previously belabored defenders of the hypothesis.

The feeling of circularity experienced by the secular person here can be explicated a little further. The secular person assumes, for whatever reasons, that the dead know nothing, and moreover that the dead can know nothing. This hypothesis is an item in his stock of beliefs. Death, for the secular person, is equated with the permanent lack of experience. But (V1) requires that a person have direct first-hand experience of an observation-sentence that is entailed by a hypothesis for the hypothesis to be verifiable. Hence the hypothesis of immortality is never verifiable at all, given the assumptions inherent in the secular world-view. Hick's arguments beg the question for the secular skeptic because they proceed from initial premises that the skeptic cannot accept without first accepting the

---

time. What this shows generally, I think, is that it is most extraordinarily difficult to avoid inconsistency when talking about death. Perhaps that is part of the explanation for our strong tendency to lapse into poetic and metaphorical language when attempting to speak about death.

hypothesis to be proved. As far as the secular person is concerned, Hick's hypothesis of immortality is not verifiable. There are no subjects (the dead) who can have first-hand experiences relevant to the verification of the hypothesis. In short, ruling out (V2) is fallacious to the person who does not already accept the religious world-view.

Of course, refusal to countenance (V2) may seem unreasonable in its own right, and we now examine the consequences of the other course of accepting both (V1) and (V2) as legitimate species of verification. This assumption provides the other horn of the dilemma. The problem here is that if Hick accepts inductive confirmation, then any hypothesis of immortality becomes falsifiable as well as verifiable.

Hick's argument that the Christian hypothesis of immortality is verifiable if true, but not falsifiable if false, is only credible if we exclude (V2) and think of verifiability solely deductively in terms of (V1). For if inductive confirmation is allowed, then certain evidence possibly available to us in this life may be allowed as confirming or disconfirming. The resurrection of Jesus, for example, could now count as inductively confirmatory evidence, But likewise, the lack of evidence of visible behavior in corpses, and rather obvious related evidence of this sort, seems to count initially against the hypothesis of survival, not to say immortality. Of course lack of evidence of visible behavior does not count against the hypothesis of disembodied survival, or against the hypothesis of relocated but embodied survival. But it does shift the burden of proof in the direction of the proponent of the hypothesis of survival. And it is just this sort of evidence of apparent vital immobility that impresses the secular skeptic strongly and plays a critical role in his thinking on death. It is a brute fact of ordinary experience that dead persons exhibit no outward signs of survival of personality, and the dissolution of the corpse and its eventual scatterment strongly suggest that the higher conscious functions do not persist. Nor would we want to entirely remove from consideration putative evidence of ESP, mediumship, mystical visions, even if such claims are familiarly open to skepticism. Now it is just because the former line of rejecting (V2) rules this kind of possible evidence out of consideration *a priori* that the skeptic feels, with justification, that there must be a sophism somewhere concealed in that line of argument.

If Hick wishes to accept (V2) then he must be able to account for this apparent preponderance of readily available counter-evidence if the Pauline conception of immortality is to be treated as anything more serious than wishful thinking. And in fact, Hick does make various suggestions that would have the effect of countering this quotidien empirical evidence. Two factors appear uppermost: (1) The resurrection body is said to be distinct from, although perhaps similar to, the physical body. Thus the fact that the physical body ceases to function does not really seem to count against this hypothesis. Moreover, the resurrection locale is a place apart from any surroundings that we are familiar with in this life, so once again, our experiences in this locale do not seem relevant. (2) The evidence for immortality is not to be sought in direct observation, but in the authority of Christ, who conveys God's promise of immortality through his word. In short, there may be additional good reasons to believe in the Christian hypothesis, but these reasons are to be found in aspects of religious insight that can only be obtained through distinctively religious sources of knowledge, such as revelation, the authority of Christ, and so forth. These areas are the real locus of confirmation or disconfirmation, and it is the epistemology of these concepts that are really at stake. I will not comment on the question of the verifiability of (1) and (2) here. I merely wish to make the clarificatory point that acceptance of (V2) requires (1) and (2) if the rather impressive quotidien evidence available to the skeptic is to be taken fairly into account, as surely it must be.

Acceptance of (V2) seems to render any hypothesis of immortality disconfirmable, or even highly disconfirmed, and so the second way of proceeding ultimately poses certain obstacles to Hick's program. This is not to say that the obstacles are insurmountable, but only that the locus of the question of verification is shifted. The question the skeptic now wishes to raise is: if the resurrection space or locale is not directly available to our experience, how can statements about it be confirmed? Here Hick needs to make a decision. Can such statements be confirmed in the sense of (V2) or not? If so, perhaps the sorts of factors mentioned in (2) are really what count. If this is so, in turn, perhaps philosophical theology should concentrate more than it has on the logic of arguments from authority as a source of religious knowledge. Are the statements of an authority verifiable? This is a critical question that has been unjustly neglected, perhaps because the structure of arguments like Hick's are such as to obscure its importance.

The Project of Resolution

The dilemma is in a way typical of arguments that take place between theologian and atheologian. Common to these disputes there is an aura of circularity. Each side displays a reluctance or inability to argue from the opponent's premises, and consequently argument takes place in a vacuum—that is to say, argument does not take place at all. Hick's insistence that the Pauline hypothesis is verifiable but not falsifiable is a case where the secular person strongly feels that somehow the question has been begged. Further analysis revealed to us an underlying ambivalence in Hick's argument that accounts for this feeling, and to some extent, explains it.

My suggestion for the eventual resolution or at least amelioration of the difficulty is to proceed on the basis that both (V1) and (V2) are acceptable and that the second horn must therefore be surmounted. In short, it seems to me that there is a strong preponderance of evidence that *prima facie* goes against the hypothesis of personal survival, and any case for immortality must be set out against this initially unfavorable basis. Accordingly, it becomes clear that the Pauline conception is a very special kind of hypothesis on immortality that has its own rather special means for confirmation quite apart from the question of the verifiability of personal survival in general. It may actually turn out to be the case that the usual kind of empirical evidence advanced by skeptics is not relevant to the Pauline hypothesis. But if so, Hick needs to show explicitly how this evidence fails to be relevant while, at the same time, the Pauline hypothesis is verifiable in principle. Moreover, it is required for Hick to establish that in demonstrating the irrelevance of this kind of evidence, he has not thereby jettisoned the verifiability of the hypothesis also.

Knowledge of Death

The dilemma tends to resist resolution because of a deeply underlying intransigency concerning the epistemology of death. It is often felt, by secular and religious thinkers alike, that it is not possible to know anything about death. After all, we do not have direct experience of death, at least while we are alive, and thus death is for us an epistemologically inaccessible state. It is often therefore assumed in a skeptical spirit that it is not possible to have any knowledge concerning death at all. Yet recently some thinkers have felt that it is possible and desirable to try to understand the phenomenon of death, and that it is possible to have some indirect knowledge of death even though, obviously, our knowledge must be limited in certain ways. Thus the need for an epistemology of death is made apparent—the epistemic limits of our knowledge of death must be made clearer.

In particular, it is important to try to understand what the relevant evidential circumstances are pertaining to the question of deciding between the religious conception of death as personal immortality and the secular conception of death as total and irrevocable extinction of consciousness. Ancillary to this question, it is necessary to understand the evidential status of the empirical evidence that is available to us now concerning death. Is this evidence entirely inconclusive or inefficacious, given the arcane aspect of death as the unexperienceable, or does it have a role to play in deliberation on death? If we can have knowledge about death, what is the nature and source of this knowledge, and what are its limits? Here is an underlying problem that reveals some of the deeper basis of the dilemma that Hick's writings suggest.

The theologian may well want to argue that various empirical propositions tend to confirm the hypothesis of personal survival. Historical evidence of the resurrection of Jesus, various forms of confirmable communication with the dead, and many other seemingly empirical claims have been made that would, if true, tend to confirm the religious conception and disconfirm the secular conception of death.[14] The atheologian might cite dissolution of the brain and central nervous system, and eventually decay and scatterment of bodily parts, as confirmatory evidence of the secular conception, equally tending to disconfirm the religious conception.[15] Both sides of the argument, citing evidence that is ostensibly empirical, have a long and varied history.[16] What I wonder, at this point, is whether the notion of eschatological verification as Hick outlines it, will remain so attractive to some theologians as a response to Flew's challenge, if it is to be defended on the empirical basis that these forms of argument suggest.

14. See Lewis (1973).
15. More details are found in Ducasse (1961) and Lamont (1952).
16. See Choron (1958).

Most of the writings on Hick's notion of eschatological verification have centered around the question of the logical consistency of the Pauline view of immortality. Issues of bodily identity in resurrection worlds have been prominent.[17] But in my experience, the real object of the skeptic's concern is not the question of consistency so much as the feeling that an enormous evasion has taken place, and that there is a very deep ambivalence underlying the whole program. I hope to have exposed that ambivalence, though I am under no illusion that it will be easy to resolve.

Religion and Fear of Death

Is it rational to fear death on the Christian hypothesis? Obviously if, according to the belief of an individual, there is a reasonable chance of eternal suffering and torture in death, then given this belief it would seem eminently reasonable, if fear is ever reasonable, to fear death. Consonant with the view that death is a punishment, we might say that fear is an integral part of the Christian attitude toward death, and more generally, toward God. Proverbs (9:10) tell us: "Principium sapientiae timor Domini." (Fear of the Lord is the beginning of wisdom.) Price (1971) suggests that a combination of fear and love, at first sight highly paradoxical, is characteristic of Christianity. Price attempts to remove the apparent contradiction by suggesting that the fear that even persists in the minds of the blessed in heaven is more like reverence or awestruck adoration. Although it still contains a sense of "belittlement," this reflects the Lord's infinite majesty, and should therefore be a cause of rejoicing (Price, 1971, p. 5).

Price argues, in addition, that fear can be desirable, and is therefore not always a completely negative emotion. There can be no real courage or self-sacrifice without fear, and the world would be insipid without fear. Moreover, fear on behalf of a loved one can be commendable. He argues (1971, p. 7) that the fear perfect love casts out is self-centered fear, but it neither can nor should cast out fear on behalf of those whom one loves.

However, the fear of the Lord, according to Price, is not pro-

17. There is quite a literature on this subject. The reader is referred to Flew (1964), Clarke (1971), Young (1970), Hick (1972), Lewis (1973), Penelhum (1970), and Purtill (1973).

tective, but may rather be pithily characterized by the phrase "sheer funk." This is the *timor Domini* which is the beginning of wisdom (according to Price, practical wisdom, or *prudentia*, rather than theoretical wisdom, or *sapientia*, strictly speaking). If Price is right, stark terror in the face of death, or more generally, in relation to God, is an integral part of the Christian's progress in religious belief, and even at the end of this progress, fear, with love, remains as a marked element of the Christian religious attitude. It is therefore quite understandable why secular thinkers like Epicurus have pointed out that religion is a major factor in promoting the idea of fear of death. On the other hand, for some, the religious conception is a consolation in the face of death. As Price (1971, pp. 82ff.) states, there are motives for disbelieving as well as believing the hypothesis of immortality. For some persons, survival may seem intolerable in whatever form it occurs, and a considerable range of reactions to the various possible alternatives is to be expected. We hasten to add that the secular and religious conceptions, as we have somewhat artificially set them out, do not exhaust, by any means, all possible viewpoints on death. Quite commonly, of course, survival is postulated in a purely secular and scientific setting of psychical research as discussed for example by Flew (1953). On this view, the element of fear so marked in the Christian view need not be present. As Price (1971, p. 88) puts it, "the ordinary decent man with no pretensions to sanctity seems to have quite a good time in the Next World, if we accept what we are told in mediumistic communications."

Chapter VII

Active and Passive Euthanasia

Recently the American Medical Association has indicated its qualified approval, under certain conditions, of some kinds of instances of what might be termed "passive" euthanasia in a statement quoted by Rachels (1975, p. 78). The need for some kind of ruling in this direction is made urgent by very pressing, widespread problems introduced by recent developments in medical technology. A characteristic instance would be the case of a terminally ill patient, who, in great pain and known to be about to die with overwhelming probability in a few days or a few hours, shows symptoms of immediately imminent death (cessation of respiration, cardiac functions, and so forth). Active, emergency methods of resuscitation are available (violent electrical shock, heart massage, and associated techniques) —a unit for this purpose is now customarily in readiness. But it is known that activation of these emergency measures will, at best, prolong the patient's life for a short and excruciatingly painful time. Moreover, as one can well imagine, repeated application of emergency resuscitation procedures in aggravated cases, where the patient could be described more as a mass of fibers than as a person, could constitute extreme cruelty. What is the physician to do? It has seemed to many that heroic measures should, under certain conditions, be waived. But does not such a waiver constitute "killing" the patient? On the other side, is not a too-strenuous interference in the course of nature equally morally abhorrent, cruel, and inhumane? The latter course may not seem to serve the interests of the patient, if unthinkingly or automatically always applied.

A possible basis for resolving these problems is said to be an often-cited distinction between "active" and "passive" euthanasia.[1] The former entails active interference in the course of natural events, the

1. For a summary of related literature and an extensive bibliography, see Gruman (1973).

taking of steps through positive action. Passive euthanasia carries with it no such requirement, but only failure to institute positive action, letting nature take its course, so to speak. Thus it is sometimes felt that passive euthanasia is morally acceptable, under certain conditions, but that active euthanasia is never morally acceptable under any conditions.

Recently, however a contravening sentiment has made itself felt, that there is really no difference between *killing* and *allowing-to-die*, and therefore the distinction between active and passive euthanasia is spurious. According to this view, if so-called "active" euthanasia is morally wrong, then cases of "passive" euthanasia cannot be without fault, since there is really no difference in principle between what appears to be the two distinct kinds of cases. This amounts to a skepticism, a denial that there is any clear difference between the two putative categories, or, if there is a difference, that it is one that can affect the basic issue. Is not to allow-to-die also to kill?

To attempt to say something constructive about this skeptical charge, we here set out what we think to be the underlying logic of the distinction between *kill* and *allow-to-die*. Specification of the minimal syntax of the distinction may aid to provide a rebuttal of the skeptic's charge that there is no clear or consistent distinction to be made at all. Second, we will show how the basic syntactical framework allows us to distinguish the logical structures of some important varieties of active and passive euthanasia. These efforts, we hope, will clarify and further solidify the distinction so that it may function as a helpful semantical tool in sorting out the obstructive complexities of the basic language of action, homicide, and euthanasia.[2]

Positive and Omissive Action

What is it to act? Von Wright[3] suggests that one answer that characterizes a singularly important type of action is this: to *act* is to *bring about* or *prevent* a change in the world (nature). According to this conception, there is a nexus of events that constitutes "nature," or natural change, and occasionally there is a disruption or interference in the natural sequence that is the result of an action on the

2. For related studies of the language of death-concepts see Kastenbaum and Aisenberg (1972).
3. See Von Wright (1968).

part of an agent who acts intentionally. An action is such that a certain state of affairs in nature would have happened, had it not been for the intervention of an agent: p was about to become true, but the agent brought it about that $\neg p$, or $\neg p$ was about to become true and the agent brought it about that p. The two paradigm instances of action could be represented symbolically as a statement-operator relativized to an individual.

(1) $\delta_a p$: a brings it about that p.

(2) $\delta_a \neg p$: a brings it about that not-p.[4]

(1) represents *productive* action, and (2) represents *preventive* action. Both represent *positive* action as opposed to omission (or forbearance) which likewise admits of two sub-varieties.

(3) $\neg \delta_a p$: a does not bring it about that p.

(4) $\neg \delta_a \neg p$: a does not bring it about that not-p.

(3) represents the case where a does not positively bring it about that p, but merely lets nature take its course, and neglects to intervene. Similarly in (4), there is no positive action as such—a merely allows p to become true in the sense of failing to reverse p. These too are kinds of action, but omissive or negative actions. The kind of action represented by (1) is stronger than that of (4), in that (1) entails (4), but not conversely. Similarly, (2) is stronger than (3), i.e., (2) entails (3), but not conversely.

The critical distinction between the pair (1), (2) on the one side, and the pair (3), (4) on the other—it is plausible to conjecture—is that the first pair (positive action) requires the actual existence of an episode of (physical) behavior to support its alleged occurrence, whereas the second pair (omission) does not. Omission can be achieved by simply "doing nothing at all." Yet this is perplexing, for how can one "do" something by "doing nothing at all"? How is inaction different from no action?

One plausible answer resides in the observation that the language of action is linked to the language of control. We allege omission to bring about a state of affairs only where we think an agent could

---

4. A more comprehensive account of the δ-operator is to be found in Pörn (1970) and Walton (1976b).

have brought about that state of affairs (had control), and also perhaps where it may have been reasonable to expect that he should have exercised his control in this case. A legal illustration may be helpful. Hart and Honoré discuss the case of *Hardcastle* v. *Bielby*, 1 Q.B. 709, 1892, where a distinction was made "between 'causing' a heap of stones to be laid upon the highway and 'allowing' it to remain there at night, to the danger of persons passing thereon."[5] The first case requires proof that the stones were laid by the accused, whereas allowing the stones to remain, it was ruled, required no positive act. Here the omission is thought to be an action because the defendant could (and should) have removed the stones. The language of action is linked to the language of control.[6] Thus a person may be said to have allowed something to happen in the sense of (4) only where he had the power to see to it that it did not happen: *a* allows *p* to obtain only if *a* controls $\neg p$. We now apply these distinctions to the case of killing.

Ways to Kill

Assume that for some individual, *b*, there is an expression, "*b* is alive" that names a state of affairs that may or may not obtain. If we place this expression for *p* in (2) and (3), a stronger and a weaker sense of "kill" are yielded. (2) becomes (2a): *a* brings it about that *b* is not alive. This is a sense of "kill" that implies, but is not implied by the weaker sense derived from (3), namely (3a): *a* does not bring it about that *b* is alive.

The interpretation of (1), (2), (3), and (4) raises a question that we now need to comment on. It may seem required, for our sense of "bring it about that *p*" to properly obtain, that *p* previously obtain. Unlike Von Wright,[7] however, we will not add that this requirement must be met. Thus (2a) need not require that *b* just previously be alive, or for that matter not alive, for *a* to bring it about that *b* not be alive. We will interpret (2a) in such a fashion that it does not specify, one way or the other, what the previous state of *b* was before the action took place. Ordinary language of action often does seem to contain this specification, but it is more convenient for our purposes

5. Hart and Honoré (1969, p. 330).
6. For more on control, see Walton (1974).
7. See note 3.

here not to include it.[8] Notice, however, that we do have the option of expressing the fuller idea of "kill" (necessarily involving a transition from "alive" to "not alive") through a conjunction, with the use of time-subscripts, and intervals $\Delta 1$ and $\Delta 2$ ($\Delta 2 > \Delta 1$). The statement of "*a* kills *b*" in this sense is: *b* was alive at *t*, and *a* brings it about at $t + \Delta 1$ that *b* is not subsequently alive: $p_t \& \delta_{a,\, t+\Delta 1} \neg p_{t+\Delta 2}$.

(1) and (4) also have interesting substitution results when "*b* is alive" is substituted for *p*, namely (1a): *a* brings it about that *b* is alive, and (4a): *a* does not bring it about that *b* is not alive. (1a) could apply in the cases where *a* saves *b*'s life, or preserves his life, or *a* resuscitates *b*. And (4a) would apply to the case where *a* forbears from killing *b*, or where *a* allows *b* to be alive.

Legal cases suggest many problematic aspects of (1), (2), (3), and (4). If *a* and *b* simultaneously shoot *c* through the heart, which one of these is true: (a) *a* brings it about that *c* is not alive; (b) *b* brings it about that *c* is not alive; (c) both; (d) neither? If *a* hurls *c* off the top of a 14-storey building and *b* shoots *c* (fatally) from a window of the 10th floor, as *c* falls, which alternative is true? And so on. Yet however we interpret δ in relation to these unspecified parameters, the basic syntactical distinction between (1), (2), (3), and (4) remains quite clear and unequivocal, as far as it goes.

Causal Analysis

Perhaps those who maintain that there is no difference between "kill" and "allow-to-die" do not mean to imply that there is literally no difference between these two expressions but only that there is no difference of causal import between them, and hence no really significant difference in regard to the responsibility that may accrue to either type of action. Accordingly, the no-difference theorist may argue that "kill" is a causal verb. McCawley's[9] celebrated analysis of the verb "kill" parses out "kill" as "cause-become-not-alive."

---

8. Thus our notation is more flexible and, in the present context, allows us to cover cases like resuscitation where the patient is "more dead than alive" and of "keeping alive." For a general discussion of this point, see Pörn (1970, ch. 1).

9. McCawley (1970).

John kills Fred

```
             S
          /  |  \
        V    NP    NP
      Cause John    |
                    S
                 /     \
               V         NP
            Become        |
                          S
                       /     \
                     V         NP
                    Not        |
                               S
                            /     \
                          V         NP
                       Alive       Fred
```

Now it is well known that causes can be negative as well as positive—
an event's not occurring may correctly be said to be the cause of
the occurrence, or non-occurrence, of another event. Thus the
operative factor in assessing responsibility for the death of Fred is
whether or not John was a causal factor in that death, and it matters
not in the least whether John's action was positive or omissive. It is
concluded that, insofar as the critical question of cause of death is
concerned, there is no significant difference, no difference that really
matters, between killing and allowing to die.

We agree that this argument is correct up to a point, that it shows,
for one thing, that both (2) and (3) are legitimate "actions" and
can both play a role in causal attributions even though (3) is
"negative." But we maintain, contrary to the foregoing argument,
that there is a difference, sometimes, in our readiness to allocate
responsibility according to whether an action is positive or omissive.
Positive action normally implies a deliberate interruption of the
course of nature, whereas allowing nature to take its course, although
a certain sanction or approval is implied—remember the connection
with control—does not carry with it such a strong imputation of

intention and deliberate agency. Of course, in both cases, the element of causation introduces the question of responsibility, but the kinds of grounds for waiving responsibility are sometimes significantly different in the two kinds of cases. Negligence, for example, is more often associated with (3) than (2).[10]

Grades of Mediated Agency

But most importantly, if we allow that a relation of causation does play a role in the language of homicide and criminal responsibility for death, we can see that we need to combine this relation of causation with (1) and (3) to understand some very significant segments of the language of euthanasia. We here introduce the symbol $\rightleftharpoons$ to represent the causal relation, here undefined[11] except for the requirement that it be irreflexive (i.e., an event never causes itself). We can now recognize that certain actions are *indirect* in the sense of culminating in the bringing about of a state of affairs only through some other state of affairs.

(5) $\delta_a q$ & $(q \rightleftharpoons p)$: *a* brings it about that *q*, and *q* causes *p*.

Any action at all can fulfill (1) (or (2), (3), or (4) if appropriate)— that is, as we understand (1), an action need not be causally unmediated to meet (1). But if an action is causally mediated, then as well as meeting (1) it also meets (5). That is, all instances of (5) are also instances of (1), but not conversely.[12] Sometimes causally unmediated actions are called "basic actions": we do not attempt to specify this class here at all, and the reader is warned not to confuse (1) with "basic action."[13] In other words, we will try not to worry

10. See Hart and Honoré (1969). The notion of a "course of nature" is at best a very difficult one in the discussion here. Professor E.-H. Kluge informs me that Ockham had some interesting things to say about it in his discussion of the argument for the existence of God adduced by Aquinas, where the latter makes use of the notion of the natural course of events.

11. Some minimal causal algebras that partially define some kinds of causal relations are found in Suppes (1970). Another source of assistance is Mackie (1965).

12. The distinctions represented by (5) to (8) are originally due to St. Anselm of Canterbury. See Henry (1967).

13. See Baier (1971).

about the admittedly very vexing problems of whether (a) causal chains originate in some isolable lower limit not itself causally med-iated, i.e., "basic" action, or (b) the causal relation is unrestrictedly transitive or whether causal chains have a "point of extinction."[14] We can now cite some varieties of indirect action. Just as (5) is an indirect counterpart to (1), indirect versions of (2), (3), and (4) are, respectively:

(6) $\delta_a \neg q$ & $(q \geqslant \neg p)$: a brings it about that not-q, and q causes not-p.

(7) $\neg \delta_a q$ & $(q \geqslant \neg p)$: a does not bring it about that q, and q causes not-p.

(8) $\neg \delta_a \neg q$ & $(q \geqslant p)$: a does not bring it about that not-q, and q causes p.

Substituting "b is not alive" for p yields four ways to "kill" in-directly.

(5a) a brings it about that q, and q causes b's not being alive.

(6a) a brings it about that not-q, and q causes b's being alive.

(7a) a does not bring it about that q, and q causes b's being alive.

(8a) a does not bring it about that not-q, and q causes b's not being alive.

In connection with euthanasia, (6a) and (7a) pertain most illustra-tively to the withholding or non-utilization of artificial life-supportive mechanisms in the case of the dying patient. (6a) represents the stronger notion whereby the support mechanism is withdrawn. (7a) represents the weaker instance, implied by (6a) but not conversely, where the support mechanism is simply not utilized at all (where it could have been used to prolong life). (5a) suggests the case where active measures are instituted to bring about death, say, by offering the patient medication that would hasten death. This would represent the highest order of active euthanasia. Finally, the case paradigmatically exemplified by (8a) is that where some life-shortening means is allowed to the patient, but where such means is not made available or administered by the agent of euthanasia (say,

14. See Suppes (1970).

the hospital staff). This might still represent what seems to be generally considered "active" euthanasia, but perhaps as "active" in a lesser degree than (5a). Similarly, (6a) and (7a) may be said to represent the two cases of passive euthanasia, where (6a) is stronger than (7a). Thus one ordering that is suggested (by no means the only one) is: (5a), (8a), (6a), (7a), in decreasing order of activeness.

A certain semantic difficulty is inherent in our approach, and requires some comment in passing. Throughout, we have used the statement variables, p, q, . . . , to stand in the syntactic categories appropriate for the entities that are related by the causal relation. In so doing, we have opted for a "propositional" approach to the causal relation, thinking informally of p and q as states of affairs (propositions, statements) that can obtain or not obtain (be true or false). There is a certain awkwardness inherent in this approach however, since a statement like "Jones pushed the button caused the factory exploded," is not well-formed. It is more natural to transform the statement into a gerundial or participial form, e.g., "Jones' pushing the button caused the explosion of the factory." In other words, many contexts are more naturally dealt with by thinking of causes and effects as "events," where, whatever an "event" is, it is something that needs to be handled differently than a proposition or statement. What is needed is a set of rules for transforming gerundial and participial expressions of a familiar kind into statements. Needless to say, however, this problem of "events" *versus* "states of affairs" is a substantial problem of the theory of action and causality, and I shall not try to take it up here, nor shall I attempt to supply the required transformation.

Concluding Remarks

There is much to be said for the skeptical intuition that the concept of action, its instance "kill," and the related concept of causation, are logically opaque, even paradoxical at certain points, and not nearly as theoretically well-behaved as we might like. It follows that the dividing line between active and passive euthanasia is bound to be blurred at critical points. We do not feel, however, that a wholesale skepticism is justified by these observations, or that one can infer from them that it is not possible to make a coherent distinction here. It is one thing to doubt that the distinction is logically coherent, and something else again to prove that it is essentially incoherent or irredeemably deviant in some specifiable way. And quite to the contrary, we have tried to show that the minimal syntax of the distinction is clear and precise, and can be laid out in a way that displays its essential logical structure. This does not mean, of course, that armed with (2a), (3a), (5a), (6a), (7a), and (8a) we can proceed to rule automatically on all cases of euthanasia. Humane, moral decisions in these cases are enormously difficult and complex in actual practice, require consideration of many medical and legal factions, and above all, depend in large part on the patient's own feelings and moral or religious point of view. But the importance and the enormous complexity of such decisions makes it imperative that the basic vocabulary of euthanasia, so often riddled with arcane inconsistencies, be made plain, clear, and minimally logically consistent, as a foundation for making intelligent and informed decisions.

The very possibility of raising skeptical doubts concerning the distinction between active and passive euthanasia shows dramatically how little we understand even the elementary logic of the language of agency, a vocabulary that is absolutely essential to a consistent, basic understanding of enormously significant moral, legal, and medical issues. That we understand little of this idiom does not, however, betoken its intrinsic incoherence, or detract from its fundamental importance.

Chapter VIII

Making-Happen and Letting-Happen

There have been a number of interesting recent developments in the formal study of the logic of human action concepts in the intensional style following the philosophical lead to Chisholm-style action theory that centers on the notion of an agent bringing about a state of affairs.[1] In my view, a main shortcoming in these formal studies is their failure to be closely coordinated with applications to actual problems of practical action. On the other side, certain applied practical problems, such as those centered around the issue of active and passive euthanasia, founder in contradiction and obscurity through the lack of any consistent and clear structure for the basic vocabulary of the general principles of human action. Admittedly, the gulf between tidy logical theory and actual messy ethical reality is wide, and such projects of bridging theory and practice mostly sound better in theory than in practice, but I hope to show that in this case a bringing together of components from both ends shows us very much better where to look for some crucial missing parts. Obviously the distinction between "killing" and "letting-die" is of as much interest to logicians, linguists,[2] and other theorists of the language of action as it is to medical and legal ethicists, but can the refinements of theory be matched to the vagaries of practice? I think that not only can it be done with highly suggestive and encouraging if not fully consolidated results but that it desperately needs to be done at this juncture. Thus in this chapter we will explore the syntactic framework of chapter VII at the semantical level.

In the first section, some relevant recent developments in the logic of action theory are very briefly adumbrated. The section, To Kill

1. See Chisholm (1964 and 1969).
2. See McCawley (1970) and Kastovsky (1973).

or Let Die, attempts to summarize, again very briefly, the relevant developments in medical ethics. To make this chapter readable by and interesting to both the informed and the uninformed, many technical refinements (more fully developed elsewhere in papers cited in the bibliography) are suppressed and various widely controversial issues of medical ethics have had to be dealt with in a cruelly abrupt fashion. I hope that the resulting deficiencies of this terse style of treatment will not completely erode the substance of this chapter. Here we strive to uncover the deeper logical structure that underlies the syntactical suggestions merely sketched in the previous chapter.

Background

Pörn (1971) has set out a logically well-written language in which an operator, "δ" ("D" in Pörn's notation), is analogous to the necessity-operator of the standard modal logic (see Hughes and Cresswell, 1968, pp. 22ff.). "$\delta_a p$" is read: a brings it about that p. This reading is made plausible by ruling (1971, p. 7) that all theorems are "brought about" and no inconsistencies are "brought about." Fitch (1963) who had earlier proposed a more minimal syntax (bringing-about is thought of as an operator closed under conjunction elimination) used the alternative device of ruling δ vacuous over theorems and negations of theorems. One difficulty with Pörn's system lies in the applicability of axiom "$\delta_a (p \supset q) \supset (\delta_a p \supset \delta_a q)$" to the idiom of action.[3] First, action-expressions are strongly and often multifariously tensed, and the "hook" is notoriously insensitive to such contexts. Judith Jarvis Thomson's type of problems are evident: if I shoot Jones at t_1 and if, as a result, he dies at t_2, when did I kill him (bring it about that he is dead)? How do we tense the third δ? Thomson (1971) shows that cogent objections can apparently be brought against any of the obvious answers. Second, there are overdetermination problems: it seems possible that according to some interpretations of "$\delta_a(p \supset q)$" that I could bring about $p_{t_1} \supset q_{t_2}$ and bring about p_{t_1} but that in the interval someone else might bring about p_{t_2} thus falsifying the axiom in question. These problems are dealt with in detail in my own work (Walton,

---

3. For an extended statement of these difficulties, see Walton (1976b).

1975) and there I suggested that the axiom, as Pörn conceives it, is inapplicable to bringing-about in the sense of "actual agency."

Perhaps through an awareness of such complications, Kanger (1972) proposed a somewhat similar logical framework, but read "$\delta_a p$" as "p is necessary for something a does." How this reading fits Pörn's axiom can be seen by interchanging the converse statements "p is necessary for q" and "q is sufficient for p" to yield "something a does is sufficient for p" as an equivalent reading. Pörn (1974) has "re-articulated" the reading to "it is necessary for something which a does that p." Making some sense of a "necessity" or "sufficiency" primitive is not much help to the action theorist however, for whom the critical problems seem to reside in the ambiguities and intransigences of these very concepts.

It has seemed to me that the best advice on how to proceed comes from the originator of the intensional style of action theory, St. Anselm of Canterbury (1033–1109). In *Lambeth Manuscript 59* (translation of 1969) he argued in effect that schemata of the form "$\neg p$" could come within the scope of the δ-operator (*non facere* is also *facere*), allowing us to distinguish among varieties of not-doing such as we might represent by the schemata "$\delta_a \neg p$," "$\neg \delta_a p$," "$\neg \delta_a \neg p$," and so forth. Concurrently, St. Anselm distinguished between direct action, "bringing it about that p" and indirect action, "bringing it about that q where q is a sufficient condition for p." As he put it (translation, 1969, pp. 229f.), an agent can bring about something itself (*facere idipsum esse*), or bring it about through some other state or affairs (*facere aliud esse*).[4]

Recent discussions of Davidson (1971) and Kim (1974) have come around to viewing the theory of action in something like an Anselmian perspective. As they see it, the main problem has a dual aspect. First, there are relations between pairs of events (or states of affairs, if you prefer these), and these relations serve to set up parallel relations between pairs of actions. Consider the relation that Davidson calls "ordinary event causation." If A causes B then if a brings it about that A, it follows that a brings it about (indirectly) that B. That there are many kinds of such relations is indicated by Goldman's treatment of varieties of such relations on tree structures in Goldman (1970), but the causal relation seems to have a special place in the priorities of action

4. See also Henry (1967).

theorists. So the first problem is to clarify these action-generating relations themselves to see how series of related actions can be formed in "chains." This is the problem of indirect action. But the second problem is the search for a semantics of bringing-about: what is it that fits into these relations and is preserved over them? A third problem, dependent on the first two and much more advanced and contentious, is that of basic action (see Danto, 1965, and Baier, 1971; Davidson, 1971, uses the term "primitive action"): do action chains have an absolute origin, are there actions that stand as the first argument in a relation to an indirect action (or a series of indirect actions) as a second element, that are not themselves second elements in the relations? To put it causally, are there bringings-about that are themselves uncaused in relation to a given sequence of bringings-about? We should note that it is possible to speak of relatively indirect action, and so try to cope with the second problem, without postulating or denying the existence of "rock-bottom" basic actions in an attempt to grapple with the third problem. In the sequel, we will attempt to concern ourselves exclusively with one aspect of the first problem, although it will prove difficult to do so while steering entirely clear of the second. On the third, we remain modestly silent.

An advanced treatment of our two problems is found in Åqvist (1974). The relation chosen by Åqvist is that of "historical necessity" as defined semantically on a game-tree, and the bringing-about notion is embedded in a formal framework that is quite helpful. Åqvist thinks of the fundamental concept of agency as a binary concept, that of an agent's *bringing something about by performing* such and such an act (Åqvist, 1974, p. 74). Again, this parallels the discussions of the "by-relation" in agency by Davidson (1971) and Kim (1974) and confirms the soundness of this Anselmian perspective. The proposal I put forward below to deal with Davidson's puzzles radically affects the scope and nature of the applicability of the Åqvist framework. Many readers will also relate the binary-relational aspect of the problem to the so-called "accordion effect" of Feinberg (1965) remarked on by Davidson (1966 and 1971): a man moves his finger, thus flicking the switch, making the light go on, illuminating the room, and warning a prowler. What we seem to have here is a set of binary relations that serve to transmit agency in a sequential fashion. Each action is indirect in relation to its predecessors.

To Omit and Not to Do

A perplexing set of problems for any theory of action concerns "negative actions": is *not-doing* also a kind of *doing?* St. Anselm's answer (1969, p. 337) was affirmative: "Pro negativis quoque verbis, etiam pro 'non facere,' ponitur saepe 'facere.' Nam qui non amat virtutes et qui non odit vitia, male facit, et qui non facit quod not debet facere, bene facit." For St. Anselm, every instance of *not-doing* is also an instance of *doing*: he who does not do what he ought not to do, does well, Thus St. Anselm's approach allows us to distinquish between $\ulcorner \delta_a \neg p \urcorner$ and $\ulcorner \neg \delta_a p \urcorner$. To illustrate the difference, if p is a good state of affairs, then $\ulcorner \delta_a \neg p \urcorner$ represents bringing about a bad state of affairs, whereas $\ulcorner \neg \delta_a p \urcorner$ merely represents failure to bring about a good state of affairs. The former implies the latter, but the converse does not obtain, and thus mere *not-bringing-about* is "weaker" than *bringing-about-not*. The Anselmian thesis that these varieties of not-doing be treated as being on a level with doing as actions is to a certain extent paradoxical because we often associate positive doing with some actual episode that is externally empirically verifiable (a hand movement or whatever) in contrast with mere not-doing which is apparently in this sense not really thought of as *action* in the same way (perhaps *inaction* or *non-action*). For many purposes, for example in the Law, it may be quite important to try to determine whether an observable episode of behavior or conduct actually occurred, but St. Anselm rules that for his purposes whether such an episode has occurred will be irrelevant. In other words, the Anselmian approach will simply fail to distinguish, one way or the other, whether any actual empirically measurable chunk of behavior has occurred—it is, so to speak, behaviorally neutral. But of course the reason that such neutrality may begin to appear paradoxical is that we do often think of the difference between *doing* and *not-doing* in terms of there being some actual behavioral episode in the former case, but not in the latter. Certainly this is a natural enough tendency and we will soon see that the deviance of the Anselmian approach from it has some philosophically interesting consequences.

To remove another source of considerable perplexity, we need also at this point to distinguish between omissions and mere non-performances. It is true that I did not just now move a certain rock in the middle of the Sahara desert, but hardly true that I omitted to do so in any sense in which I might be said to be responsible for my non-action. That is, there is a sense of *omit* for which more than mere not-doing is required. If we say, for example, that I omitted to move a pile of stones from the roadway with the result that a vehicle was damaged, we might imply that not only did I not remove the stones, but I had control over their removal and failed to act. Here we postulate a distinction between action and action-control in such a way that it is sometimes true to say that I did something but did not control my action (in the sense of bodily control whereby I do control my giving you the money even though you have a gun at my temple). Some action theorists seem inclined to think that something is an action of mine if and only if I have bodily control over it, but we will use the term "control" here in such a way that I may be sometimes said to bring about states of affairs over which I had no control at the time, for example, a sneeze might be an action of this kind. (See Rescher, 1969, and Walton, 1974 and 1976a, for more on control.)

Likewise we might assume that there are some states of affairs that we do not bring about but do control their being brought about, and these we might call *omissions*. Thus omissions are a subclass of not-doings, names those not-doings whose doing was under the control of the agent at the time. Thus I omitted to move the rocks because I didn't move them but I did have control over moving them.[5]

Not much need turn on the concept of control in our discussion here, but I think it is important to see that the Anselmian notion of not-doing is not vacuous, because it can be utilized in conjunction with other components of a theory of action, such as the concept of "control," to move towards a richer theory more adequate to fuller notion of an omission.

Making-Happen and Letting-Happen

One species of not-doing is of particular interest, namely that represented by the scheme $\ulcorner \neg \delta_a \neg p \urcorner$, read as "*a* does not bring it about that not-*p*." Another reading for this might be "*a* lets *p* occur" or "*a* allows *p* to occur," in the sense of *a*'s not bringing it about that *p* does not obtain.[6] This too, on the Anselmian approach is a kind of "action": perhaps it might be called *passive action* as opposed to the

---

5. Compare Åqvist (1974, p. 81).
6. This notion is a development from chapter VII.

active variety of agency represented by $\ulcorner \delta_a p \urcorner$. Since my letting p occur while not myself actively bringing it about that p,

$$\neg \delta_a \neg p \ \& \ \neg \delta_a p$$

is a consistent state of affairs, it follows that letting p obtain $(\neg \delta_a \neg p)$ does not entail bringing p about $(\delta_a p)$. However, since bringing about p is presumably inconsistent with bringing about not-p (at the same time), it is in general true that bringing about p entails letting p obtain.

$$\delta_a p \supset \neg \delta_a \neg p$$

Thus bringing about is a stronger form of agency than letting-happen.[7] In this respect, δ and $\neg \delta \neg$ are like the L and M of normal modal logic. Analogously, let us introduce an abbreviated form of the notion of letting-happen by the definition,

$$\zeta_a p \ =_{df} \ \neg \delta_a \neg p$$

Thus $\ulcorner \zeta_a p \urcorner$ is to be read as "a lets it happen that p." Of course we will have to be quite clear that a deontic sense of "allow" or "permit" is not meant, nor the sense of "let happen" that has to do specifically with the control of actions. (See Walton, 1974.)

Now this way of characterizing the praxic "let" has an immediate consequence of philosophical significance. For, by double negation, we obtain the equivalence, $\ulcorner \delta_a p \equiv \neg \zeta_a \neg p \urcorner$, which doubly underlines the warning that, in the Anselmian theory, action should not be thought of in terms of actual episodes of behavior. The reasoning that leads up to this conclusion runs as follows. First, it is quite plausible to think that I can not-let-something-not-happen without actually engaging in any overt behavior, but by simply being prepared to intervene, should the need arise. For example, suppose Smith is in the process of shooting Jones. I could stop the process if I wished, but quite the contrary, I am determined to intervene if Smith should falter. Moreover assume that Smith knows that if I shoot Jones I will also shoot him, Smith, since I am in the habit of eliminating witnesses to my crimes. Note that I need not exhibit any "overt behavioral episodes" at the time, but I do nevertheless, in a very plain and obvious way, not let it happen that Jones is not shot. Now according to our equivalence, $\ulcorner \delta_a p \equiv \neg \zeta_a \neg p \urcorner$, it is true to say, in this case, that I bring it about that Jones is shot. This conclusion

7. We return to this idea in the section, Moral Evaluation of Actions.

seems paradoxical, however, because I did not, from a point of view of overt behavior, do anything, and it would certainly be false to say that I shot Jones. We seem to have the absurd consequence that I can bring something about without doing anything!

The sting of this consequence is lessened, of course, by being more specific about times of actions. I can bring about something at t even though I engage in no overt activity at t if at some earlier time t', I did something that resulted in something else that occurred at t. Bringing in the complexities we noted earlier in the first section pertaining to chains of action and multiply tensed actions puts a different complexion on the problem, yet there remains a natural inclination to insist that if a genuine action has occurred, somewhere along the line a chunk of actual overt behavior must have entered in. Still, in all, I think there is an important lesson in our consequence, namely that on the Anselmian theory of action, whether or not an individual a has brought something about simply yields no information whatever on the question of whether there has been an actual overt bodily movement by a.

Admittedly it is hard to know exactly how we might define "actual overt bodily movement." If this expression is construed widely enough to include neuron impulses in the brain, for example, then I would certainly have to retract the thesis of Anselmian behavior-neutrality. Suffice it to say that there does seem to be a narrower construal of the expression in question that pinpoints an interesting limitation of the Anselmian language, even if that limit is vague. It is often felt, naturally enough, that the difference between "bringing-about" and "letting-happen" resides in the consideration that in the former case, but not in the latter, there is a positive, actual, chunk of behavior directly involved. On the Anselmian theory, this need not be so. What then, on the Anselmian account, is the difference? Here is a question of some significance, as the next section will show. We have now given a partial answer, but carry it further in the section, Anselmian Semantics.

To Kill or Let Die

We recall here that while some distinction like that between active and passive euthanasia is widely operative in the practice of medical decision making, it is the feeling of some commentators that the basis of the distinction is obscure, elusive, or even trivial.[8] Factors included in making the problem prominent are the development of resuscitation technology, and especially techniques for artificial ventilation. Thus it is often said that withdrawal of treatment "under extraordinary circumstances" from a patient who will consequently die somewhat earlier than he otherwise would, should be allowed under certain conditions even if "active" or "positive" intervention is intolerable in any circumstances. We also saw that many critics feel there is no real difference between active and passive euthanasia or only a trivial distinction (Morison, 1973).

A second problem that forces the need to explore the issue is that of children with meningomyeloceles. Freeman (1972) argues that since in deciding to treat or not, the physician is making a decision between life and death, why should the physician not also have the opportunity to take active measures to alleviate suffering?[9] What is the basis for accepting passive euthanasia but condemning active intervention if the latter appears the more humane alternative?

The natural response is that active euthanasia involves an overt episode of conduct whereas passive euthanasia does not. In flat contradiction, however, we have it that turning off a ventilator, an act usually thought to characterize only passive euthanasia, is an actual episode of conduct. What seems the natural basis of the distinction is simply untenable. Thus we are challenged to find an alternative basis for the distinction, if one exists.

What is needed is a basis for the distinction that is significant from a moral point of view. So far, no such basis is yielded by the literature on this subject, to our knowledge. Kluge (1975, p. 156) writes:

> The argument is sometimes made in medical circles, that there is a difference between permitting a patient to die by abstaining from the use of extraordinary means of prolonging his life and actually killing him. There is no question that there is a difference between the two sorts of acts. However, it is a difference which, from a moral point of view, is inconsequential. Physically, the two sets of acts are distinct. Morally, they have the same status since, from a moral point of view, failure to do something is also to do something; the absence of an act is also an act. This moral fact lies at the basis of the legal concept of

8. See Morison (1973), Rachels (1975), Freeman (1972), and Habgood (1974).
9. Compare the remarks of Rachels (1975) on Down's syndrome.

culpable negligence: the failure to perform an act which, morally speaking, the individual was duty bound to do. Therefore, whether the euthanasia practice consists in an overt act of killing or the withdrawal (or refusal to administer) life-support systems, the moral status of these procedures are on the same level. Nothing is solved by pointing to their physical difference. The real issue—the moral issue—is still to be decided.

Kluge displays a skepticism—there is a difference, but it is one that is morally inconsequential. Is there a difference of genuine moral import then? Nothing is resolved by citing the obvious physical difference between the two kinds of cases. Michael Tooley (1972 and 1976) even goes so far as flatly to deny that there is any difference of moral import, and formulates a Moral Symmetry Principle to express his conjecture:

> Let C be a causal process that normally leads to outcome E. Let A be an action that initiates process C, and let B be an action that stops process C before outcome E occurs. Assume further that actions A and B do not have any other morally significant consequences, and that E is the only part or outcome of process C which is morally significant in itself. Then there is no moral difference between performing action A, and intentionally refraining from performing action B, assuming identical motivation in the two cases. (Tooley, 1976, p. 31.)

According to Tooley, the distinction is simply based on either confused thinking or a "taboo" morality. He cites many instances that, like Rachels' example, suggest strongly that insofar as we think of "bringing-about" in purely physicalistic terms, not allowing "background factors" like motivations, intentions, and so on, to play a role, letting-happen is equally culpable, no more nor less culpable than positive bringing-about. Is offering poison to a person more wrong than allowing him to consume poison and intentionally refraining from administering the antidote which one has in his pocket? So far as the motives, intentions, and other background factors are held constant and equal in both cases, Tooley argues that there can be no moral difference. The Anselmian syntax of chapter IV suggests a different possible basis of differentiation than the one Tooley seems to presuppose, but what reason do we have to think that this new possible basis for differentiation is any more significant from a moral point of view than the mere physical difference? To lead up to this question, we next attempt to focus our moral intuitions on a specific example, a paradigm that will, I hope, make the issue clearer and more concrete. Through this paradigm we will introduce a new and somewhat unexpected basis for the kind of distinction that Kluge seeks.

The Case of the Drowned Cousin

To investigate whether there is really any difference between killing and letting-die, Rachels (1975, p. 79) considers two cases that, he postulates, are exactly alike except that one involves killing and the other letting-die.

> In the first, Smith stands to gain a large inheritance if anything should happen to his six-year-old cousin. One evening while the child is taking his bath, Smith sneaks into the bathroom and drowns the child, and then arranges things so that it will look like an accident. In the second, Jones also stands to gain if anything should happen to his six-year-old cousin. Like Smith, Jones sneaks in planning to drown the child in his bath. However, just as he enters the bathroom, Jones sees the child slip and hit his head, and fall face down in the water. Jones is delighted; he stands by, ready to push the child's head back under if necessary, but it is not necessary. With only a little thrashing about, the child drowns by himself, "accidentally," as Jones watches and does nothing.

Rachels postulates that both men acted from the same motive, and both had the same end in view. In both cases, the consequences are identical. How could we say that one man acted better or worse than the other? It would hardly be a reasonable defence for Jones to plead that he was less guilty because he didn't actually do anything, that he merely let the child die. Thus how can it be, challenges Rachels, that letting-die is less bad than killing? The bare difference of killing and letting-die seems to make no difference, certainly no difference of obvious moral significance. Letting-die constitutes "the intentional termination of life" (Rachels, 1975, p. 78) too and is therefore equally serious in ethical import. Rachels' case constitutes a direct challenge to put forward a rational basis for the distinction that can elucidate how, if at all, there is a difference between killing and letting-die that is of import in the weighting of responsibility or blameworthiness. The skeptic can use this case to document clearly his contention that there is no evident, discernible difference to be made out, and a defender of the distinction had better be able to show, specifically in this test case, just where the difference lies and how it can be clearly explicated.

Anselmian Semantics

In chapter VII, and further in the section Making-Happen and Letting-Happen, we postulated a syntactic framework for "make-happen" and "let-happen" that obviously has some bearing on Rachels' challenge. But a required step for the application of this syntax is its interpretation. Therefore let us adumbrate a semantic structure for Anselmian "bringing-about" and "letting-happen." To do this, we think of a proposition p as included in a set of possible outcomes that may either obtain or not obtain at a time t'. Then the semantical rule for δ, relative to an agent, a, reads as follows: $\delta_{a,t}p_{t'}$ is true if, and only if, $p_{t'}$ is true in every possible outcome at t' relative to agent a at t.[10] The semantical rule for ζ reads: $\zeta_{a,t}p_{t'}$ is true, if and only if, $p_{t'}$ is true in at least one possible outcome at t' relative to a at t. Accordingly, a is thought to bring p about where a allows no other outcome inconsistent with p, where a makes p happen in the sense of shaping the world so that no outcome that excludes p can ensue. We might paraphrase this notion as "a ensures that p will happen" or "a arranges things so that no reasonable alternative to p can occur." a is thought to let p happen, according to this interpretation, where a allows room for p, but other outcomes (possibly) as well, where a lets p happen in the sense of shaping the world so that p is enabled to occur. This might be paraphrased as "a allows p to happen" or "a provides a necessary condition for the occurrence of p" just as "a makes p happen" is meant in the sense of "a provides a sufficient condition for the occurrence of p." What we have in mind here is the picture of a set of possible outcomes at t' that are accessible to the actual state of the world at "the previous instant" t.

10. Compare Pörn (1971, pp. 11ff.), Kanger (1972, p. 121) and Åqvist (1974, p. 74f).

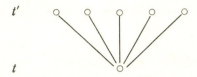

If p is included in all the outcomes at t' relative to an agent a, then a makes p happen. If p is included in at least one possible outcome relative to a, then a lets p happen. Many details of this sketch need filling in, but let us concentrate on dealing with those obviously relevant to our present needs.

According to how we view the accessibility relation, stronger and weaker notions of "make-happen" and "let-happen" are apparent. For example, we might consider adding the axioms characteristic of S5 and S4 respectively,

$$\zeta_a p \supset \delta_a \zeta_a p$$
$$\delta_a p \supset \delta_a \delta_a p$$

to characterize a stronger notion of "let" (active letting) and a stronger notion of "bring-about." Neither notion, on the Anselmian approach, is entirely univocal or simple. Tensing also leads to many complexities essential to agency. But most important for our purposes here are questions of multiple-agent bringing-about and letting-happen. If you and I, each carrying a lighted candle, simultaneously enter a gas-filled sewer that consequently explodes, it would be correct to say that we jointly brought about the explosion, i.e., what I did ensured it and what you did ensured it. This schema would be appropriate.

$$\delta_a p \ \& \ \delta_b p$$

Note therefore that the above schema is not inconsistent on the Anselmian semantics. That is, the Anselmian theory allows for over-determination of agency. In other significantly dissimilar cases of what might also be called "joint agency" the individual action of each agent is required to bring about the state of affairs in question, e.g., where you and I jointly move a large rock that neither of us could individually move. Here the above schema would not be true, rather, it was our "conjunctive" or "union-agency" that ensured the rock's moving.

$$\delta_{a \& b} p$$

Here, semantically speaking, you and I jointly saturated the possible outcomes with p.

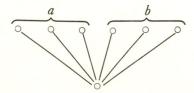

In this case it is also true that each of us let p happen. In a true case of joint agency of this second type each agent must be such that he let p occur (each agent is required to effect the outcome).

$$\zeta_a p \ \& \ \zeta_b p$$

Here we have two kinds of two-person interpersonal agency that need to be clearly distinguished. Let us call them respectively *dual agency* (overdetermination case) and *joint agency* (both agents required). The second might also be called *joint agency proper*.

Before applying this semantical sketch to the problem in hand, two philosophical points should be stressed. First, it should be quite clear that, as Anselmian bringing-about is here conceived, bringing something about need not require any overt behavior on the part of the agent at the time what is brought about occurs. Indeed, as we saw earlier, Anselmian agency is simply neutral in regard to the question of whether any external empirical behavior-episode has or has not taken place. But now we have given a semantical interpretation of δ and ζ, this point should be clearly apparent. Second, there is a natural tendency in the language of agency often to think of Nature as being an agent (or pseudo-agent) analogous to a human agent (Anthropomorphism?).[11] As far as the Anselmian theory is concerned, this way of speaking is perfectly all right, since we have not laid down any constraint on what can constitute an agent, and there is no *prima facie* reason to exclude non-human agents (e.g., animals, traffic lights, computers, etc.). But speaking of Nature as an agent has a consequence that is significant for our problem. To see this consequence, observe first that while $\ulcorner \delta_a p \supset p \urcorner$ is an axiom for Anselmian bringing about, $\ulcorner \zeta_a p \supset p \urcorner$ is not. Simply because I let something happen in the Anselmian sense, it does not follow that it will happen. (If this seems odd, remember the semantics for ζ.) But

11. Note Åqvist (1974, p. 84).

if something *does* happen in a case where I let it happen and, as far as we know no other agent made it happen, then it is quite natural to think of Nature as the joint agent who completed the action of bringing it about.

Finally, I would like to remark on a problem of agency that I have been unable to solve yet in the Anselmian framework developed so far. I think it is true that sometimes in a case of joint agency we tend to think of one agent as being the dominant or principal agent and the other as more of a supporter or accessory agent. What I have in mind to correspond with this notion in the Anselmian model is a set of outcomes where a (the supporter) let p occur, i.e., includes p in some possible outcomes, and b then saturates all the other outcomes with p.

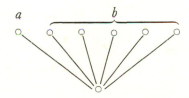

What sort of parameters determine dominance in joint agency is at present, however, still obscure to me. Some interesting suggestions are found in Åqvist (1974). It occurs to me that one context where a is said to act jointly with b at t where a's act is dominant is that in which a's act would have brought about p at some time not long after t even without b's enabling the outcome p at t. But I will not pursue this or other like suggestions further here.

Analysis of Rachels' Paradigm

Now we are ready to reconsider the case of the drowned cousin set by Rachels. How will the Anselmian language of making and letting happen allow us to explicate the distinction between Smith, who drowns the child, and Jones, who stands by in readiness, but needs to make no drowning motion to accomplish his fell purpose? Surprisingly, it is quite clear that the Anselmian theory must rule that both Smith and Jones brought about the drowning of their respective nephews! For Jones, every bit as much as Smith, has not allowed any other outcome than the drowning. Rachels' description of the case of Jones makes this evident: "Jones is delighted; he stands by, ready to push the child's head back if necessary . . . " The counterfactual especially underlines the thesis that Jones made it happen that the child was drowned, in the sense of forcing it to happen, in the sense of allowing no possible alternative outcome: "If the child had not drowned (without Jones' pushing it under), Jones would have ensured this outcome (by pushing it under)." By Rachels' description of the postulated case, this counterfactual is clearly meant to be true. Thus in both the cases of Smith and Jones, the agent brought the drowning about, rather than merely letting it happen. But as surprising as this ruling may initially seem, we should have been prepared for it by our previous warnings that the Anselmian theory is neutral with regard to the question of actual overt behavior. Perhaps there was overt behavior on the part of Jones, perhaps not; the Anselmian theory is not affected either way in its ruling on whether a bringing-about or mere letting-happen occurred.

Notice however that we may not make a direct inference from the statement that Jones brought it about that the child was drowned to the statement "Jones drowned the child" or the statement "Jones killed the child." I do not think that everyone would object to drawing this inference, but I feel that the latter statements are too closely linked to some actual motion of drowning, some actual episode of conduct, to make the inference free from an air of paradox. Rather "Jones killed the child" or "Jones drowned the child" seem, at least in some aspects of their usage in natural language, linked to Jones' bringing-about of the state of affairs of the child's drowning by means of some actual bodily movement. Despite this admission however, it is well to observe that there are a plurality of rough edges to the notion of human actions (often brought out in legal cases of homicide, for example) that could only adequately be dealt with if we extend our theory much further than we are able to here. Does Jones kill the child (drown the child) if he throws a baseball that hits the child on the head and drowning ensues—if he convinces Schmidt to drown the child—if the baseball hits Schmidt who, in an induced fit of lunacy, drowns the child? And so on. These sorts of contingencies suggest that simply equating "bringing-about" with "action" would be premature: there are too many exotic "actions" to deal with without much more elaboration of the Anselmian theory, something we will not attempt further here.[12]

Nevertheless, the Anselmian theory does give us a clear basis for contrasting the simpler cases of bringing-about and letting-happen, and moreover it yields the highly significant result of supporting Rachels' intuition that there is no genuine difference between the cases of Smith and Jones. This is an exciting result because it meets Rachels' challenge, or at least goes a step towards meeting it. Rachels argues that in the case he outlines, there is no difference in moral responsibility between "killing" and "letting-die." The Anselmian theory rules that, as far as it goes, there is likewise no difference—both are cases of "making a death happen" rather than merely letting it occur. As we saw in the sections, To Omit and Not to Do and Making-Happen and Letting-Happen, the preanalytically natural approach, in contrast, would rule that there is a characteristic difference between killing and letting-die that marks the crucial difference between the cases of Smith and Jones—in the first case, but not the second, an actual bodily movement, a behavioral episode of a certain kind, actually occurred. What I am suggesting is that the Anselmian theory squares better with the rational allocation of moral responsibility in Rachels' case than the natural approach. What is most important from a viewpoint of moral responsibility may not be, in this paradigm case and other similar cases, the question of whether some actual bodily movements occurred at the time, but whether there was a "making-happen" as opposed to a "letting-happen" according to the Anselmian theory.

I hasten to add that not all cases are by any means similar in all respects to Rachels' paradigm from a point of view of ethical accountability, and that, therefore, whether or not an actual bodily movement of a certain kind in the spatio-temporal vicinity of what is done may be of critical moral significance—certainly such actual behavior is crucial in legal deliberations. But I am suggesting that the Anselmian account has some remarkable and worthwhile advantages over the natural account, as a theoretical basis of the distinction between making-happen and letting-happen.

12. But see Walton (1976b). Some related problems are dealt with in a forthcoming paper, "Pure Tensed Action Propositions," in the context of difficulties suggested by Davidson (1966).

Active and Passive Euthanasia

What light do these abstractions throw on the physicians' dilemma of active and passive euthanasia? My response is that the Anselmian approach gives us a basis grounded in logic for vindicating the legitimacy of the often but hazily drawn distinction between active bringing-about and passive letting-happen. It does not effect the distinction in what we have called the "natural" way, but consideration of Rachels' challenge, I propose, shows this to be an advantage rather than a shortcoming. Indeed, what seems the natural way of drawing the distinction is, I think, highly dubious. As has often been noticed, in actual cases of what is thought of as passive euthanasia, there are behavioral episodes and bodily movements, e.g., turning off the ventilator. Similarly, in Rachels' paradigm case, even in the alleged "passive" case, instances of actual conduct may be attributable to Jones, i.e., standing in an attitude of readiness and so forth. Rather, the Anselmian approach suggests drawing the distinction between active and passive euthanasia from an entirely different point of view.

According to the Anselmian approach, to make something happen is to ensure that outcome, virtually, to force that outcome on nature (or other agents) by, in effect, blocking all outcomes that do not contain the state of affairs brought about. A paradigm of Anselmian bringing-about of death might be, for example, a fatal injection of a highly toxic substance. Metaphorically speaking, "Nature is left no alternative": more exactly, every alternative outcome accessible to the actual world in which the poison is injected is such that a death of the patient occurs.

Now we come to the question of letting-die. What that consists in is clearly explicated by the Anselmian semantics—at least one outcome (but not necessarily every outcome) accessible to the actual world of the agent is such that a death of the patient occurs in that outcome—but whether a case of turning off a ventilator, or allowing a baby with Down's syndrome to die of an intestinal obstruction or renal infection is always as genuine a case of Anselmian letting-die is, in my opinion, not a straightforward matter. I do think, however, that the Anselmian semantics does throw some light on the underlying logical basis of how such a decision might rationally be made, and thereby clarifies a critical pivot of the distinction that has heretofore been arcane. I think the critical point is this. If turning off a ventilator, for example, is such that every possible outcome relative to the agent is one in which the death of the patient occurs, then death has been brought about. But if the turning off of a ventilator amounts only to making possible the death of the patient while at the same time leaving open other possible alternative outcomes for Nature or another agent to pursue, then merely a "letting-die" is entailed. But how in turn are we to make this decision? The Anselmian theory does not tell us, of course; it merely makes the question somewhat more precise and pointed.

But the Anselmian theory does reorient our thinking on this matter. In a genuine case of passive euthanasia, it is not that the doctor "does nothing" as is often incorrectly (but naturally) thought. (See Rachels, 1975, p. 80.) On the contrary, according to the Anselmian account, letting-happen is also a species of action itself, and, for that matter, as we saw, may also be accompanied by overt behavior. Accordingly, letting a patient die, is not "no action at all" and may therefore be open to moral appraisal just as bringing about something may entail responsibility.

Moral Evaluation of Actions

Both bringing-about and letting-happen may be open to moral evaluation and responsibility, but is the former more culpable than the latter? Certainly any moral judgement is strongly tied to a particular context and situation, but the Anselmian theory confirms our intuitive judgement of the greater strength and seriousness of the former in many situations by ruling that bringing-about implies letting-happen whereas the converse does not obtain, i.e., it is a theorem that

$$\delta_a p \supset \zeta_a p$$

whereas the converse cannot be a theorem. Such is clearly dictated by our semantics since if p is in all outcomes then it will be in at least one outcome. Also, bringing-about is conclusive, i.e.,

$$\delta_a p \supset p$$

is an axiom whereas $\ulcorner \zeta_a p \supset p \urcorner$ is not. Consequently, of course $\ulcorner \delta_a p \supset \zeta_a p \urcorner$ is an axiom. Thus bringing-about is "stronger than" letting-happen. We stress again, however, that this by no means implies that letting-happen is, on the Anselmian account, always morally unexceptionable. While this account does drive a wedge between active and passive euthanasia, it does not do so to the extent of yielding a blanket sanction of passive euthanasia.

Why is bringing-about thought, *ceteris paribus*, to be more serious than letting-happen or more culpable from a point of view of moral responsibility? The Anselmian theory suggests an answer. To bring something about is in effect to exert greater force on the natural flow of events by shaping them in such a fashion that a certain outcome must occur—Nature (or Society) is left no alternative. But to let something happen is to leave open alternatives, from a viewpoint of the agent himself, even if Nature or Society should carry through the outcome enabled by the agent anyway. In letting something happen, an agent leaves alternatives open to the world external to his *aegis*. This is especially apparent in interpersonal cases—I can enable you to do something without actually seeing to it myself that the thing is done. I can leave it up to you. Thus, letting-happen is less forceful shaping of the world, a leaving-open of channels of development and agency that themselves are forces that contribute to a shaping of events.[13]

At bottom, I feel that we tend to think passive euthanasia less culpable because we conceive of Nature as the dominant agent in these cases—the physician merely lets happen what Nature inevitably brings about. We have seen however that the concept of *dominant agent* and *Nature as agent* are at present mere metaphors not yet well

---

13. The remarks in Moral Evaluation of Actions leave us open to the following charge: we can never make an absolute moral judgement for a given case because we can never know, short of universal knowledge of state-descriptions of the universe and its laws, what possibilities are open. Thus "x brings it about that p" will always carry the rider "relative to our knowledge of the universe." This possibly unwelcome consequence can however be lessened by leaving open the option of interpreting the "possible worlds" of our framework as possible states of knowledge of an agent at a given time. Thus "possibilities" can be thought of in an "epistemic" as well as an "ontic" way. This dual interpretation of our theory, first suggested to me by J. Michael Dunn, is brought out more perspicuously in chapter X. A similar criticism of the Anselmian account of bringing-about in terms of the exclusion of other states of affairs might be suggested by the highly plausible remark that one can never really exclude all possibilities. To be able to do so would seem to imply complete control over the universe, in some sense. This criticism is dealt with in chapter X.

defined or understood in the Anselmian theory. Here are some notions worth exploring.

Concluding Remarks

The above developments and applications of the Anselmian approach in connection with the question of making-happen and letting-happen represent stronger confirmation of the hypothesis suggested by the discussion of the axiom $\ulcorner \delta_a(p \supset q) \supset (\delta_a p \supset \delta_a q)\urcorner$, namely that the notion of bringing-about as developed within a T-logic[14] (pursued by Pörn, 1971 and 1974, and Kanger, 1972, and partially followed out in the present treatment and otherwise discussed elsewhere by myself in Walton, 1976b), is not applicable to a strong sense of "actual agency" that implies an episode of overt behavior, but is more satisfactorily applied through an interpretation like that suggested here. That is, to bring about a state of affairs is to "ensure" its occurrence, to not allow possible outcomes that do not include that particular state of affairs. Now one might think this somewhat extraordinary view of bringing-about would be trivial or uninteresting when applied to practical problems of action, but our findings here have been quite to the contrary. For one way of interpreting Rachels' paradigm is that whether or not there is an episode of overt behavior (of a familiar if difficult to define type— some sort of bodily movement) in the immediate spatio-temporal vicinity of what is done does not constitute a factor that is essentially relevant to the evaluation of moral responsibility. This suggests that the Anselmian account may be a better candidate than what we called the "natural" approach for the analysis of the kind of bringing-about that is relevant to contexts of moral responsibility, especially in the context of the contrast between making-happen and letting-happen. Finally, I tried to show how the Anselmian account throws some light on the distinction between active and passive euthanasia. Here we were less successful—first, because the problem itself is so widely ramified, but second, because this distinction appears to depend to a large extent on aspects of the Anselmian theory not yet developed in an exact fashion. Nevertheless, I think our results do go some way to meeting Rachels' challenge by yielding a basis for the distinction developed far beyond any existing treatment. Obviously, however, much remains to be done.

14. See the treatment of Hughes and Cresswell (1968, chs. 2 and 4).

Chapter IX

Groundwork for a Typology of Elective Death

In recent literature in medical ethics distinctions are made, such as those between *active* and *passive* euthanasia and *direct* and *indirect* euthanasia, that are not, at any rate exclusively, moral or juris-prudential, but that pertain to the underlying logic of human action.[1] At present much confusion surrounds these kinds of dis-tinction, even to the extent that a considerable skepticism has accrued against the claim that they can be drawn in a clear or helpful way that indicates their relevance to moral evaluation. I will attempt briefly to indicate here how a general groundwork for a typology to frame a set of such distinctions can be formulated in a way that is useful in systematizing the language of euthanasia. The theses I propose are of course "merely semantical," but I hope to show by applying them to some work of Fletcher (1973) that they are well worth formulating in connection with the concept of euthanasia, as a contribution to what is thought of as the conceptual or philosophical level of inquiry of medical ethics by Cassell, Kass, et al. (1972) and McCormick (1974) In chapters VII and VIII, the logic underlying the typology developed here is more specifically directed towards the clarification of the distinction between active and passive euthanasia. In this chapter, the primary object of study will be direct and indirect euthanasia. For those to whom the term "euthanasia" is objectionable or problematic, what we seek might better be captured by Fletcher's phrase "a typology of elective death."

---

1. An interesting discussion of the relation of analytic to valuative thinking in medicine that helps to clarify some possible misconceptions of the kind of project attempted here is presented by Cassel (1975).

Indirect Action

We begin by outlining some distinctions drawn from the general theory of human action. We do not pretend that these distinctions themselves are not uncontroversial within action theory, but we do contend that they have been sufficiently developed to make their application to practical problems of medical ethics a benefit to both theory and practice. Certainly we make no claims of substantiating a comprehensive theory of action here or of providing specific localized decision procedures for the highly ramified, situational, life-or-death dilemmas of modern medical practice. Yet the pioneering work of Fletcher (1973) points the way in its clear indication that general principles of human agency are critically and centrally involved at the conceptual level, and must be further explicated if a rational basis for discussion and evaluation is to be forthcoming. The outline of the relevant action theory that follows is, of necessity, a bare heuristic sketch, and readers are referred to the works cited for a more adequate account. See also the section, Making-Happen or Letting-Happen, of chapter VIII for an account of this background literature.

An agent a will be said to bring about an event B R-*indirectly* where there is some event A, distinct from B, that stands in a relation R to B. There may be many kinds of R-relations, but an often-cited and illustrative one is the causal relation.[2] Thus we could say that a brings about B *causally indirectly* where a brings about some event A (distinct from B) and A causes B. To illustrate: I brought it about causally indirectly that the window was broken because there was something that I brought about that caused the breaking of the window, namely the motion of a stone through the air. Sometimes also R-relations can link sequences of events so that if A stands in a certain R-relation to B and B stands in the same relation to C, then if I bring about A, I am likewise said to bring about C (indirectly). Thus some R-relations are transitive over certain sequences of events, but how to characterize the length of such sequences is a question we will not go into.[3] We seem often to want to require that

2. For some applications to the health sciences, see Susser (1973). The groundwork adumbrated here will, I hope, encourage not only theoretical refinements of the language, but also work at the practical levels in applying this language to substantive problems of medical ethics.

3. For fuller discussion, the reader should look to the work of Kim (1974) and Davidson (1971).

two events must be distinct in order to be *R*-related, but whether this is generally true of *R*-relations, or whether this indicates that *R*-relations are irreflexive, would require much more analysis of both such relations and the highly problematic concept of an event.

R-relationality is similar to the notion of level-generation of Goldman (1970). Some examples cited by Goldman are not causal, e.g., I put my hand out the car window and thereby (indirectly) signal a turn. Here the *R*-relationship pertains to certain conventions concerning traffic signalling. Certain interpersonal transactions also seem to share an element of convention. If captain *a* orders private *b* to bring about *B*, then there is some (perhaps not very clear) sense in which *a*, in giving the order, has himself indirectly brought it about that *B*. Here the *R*-relation has to do with the "chain of command."

The distinction between direct and indirect agency is due to St. Anselm of Canterbury who, in *Lambeth Manuscript 59* (translation of 1969), distinguished between an action that is brought about through some other action (*per aliud*) and an action that is brought about through itself (*per se*). For example, a person can bring about the death of another directly (by stabbing) or indirectly, by giving the killer a knife, or by disarming the victim. For St. Anselm, indirect "actions" are to be thought of as actions as well, even though they do not seem to be as closely related to actual bodily movements as are direct actions.

An extended discussion of the logic of indirect agency is given in Walton (1976c), but discussions of specific candidates for *R*-relations are found in Chisholm (1969), causality; Åqvist (1974), "historical necessity" (defined on a game-tree); Kanger (1972), sufficient conditionality. The logic of indirect agency is, of course, an ongoing problem of action theory, and the details of its analysis remain in a state of flux, but perhaps we have outlined the basic idea clearly enough that the applicability of it to the question of euthanasia may be seen.

Fletcher's Topology

It has become well known that what amounts to euthanasia (passive euthanasia) has become a practice in modern hospitals due to the development of technology (e.g., ventilating machines) that allows life to be sustained temporarily under hopeless, heroic, and inhumane conditions.[4] What amounts to passive euthanasia has also been part of medical practice in connection with deformities in infants such as meningomyloceles.[5] Given widespread recognition of these practices, and given the basic obscurity of the ethical terminology involved, certain ethical dilemmas involving the definition of "euthanasia" and classification of its varieties have evolved, e.g., it is argued by Freeman (1972) and Rachels (1975) that since there is no clear or morally relevant distinction between active and passive euthanasia, if the latter is allowed, the former should also be permitted. In order to help clarify the taxonomical and semantical entanglements that have been produced by these substantive ethical dilemmas, Fletcher (1973) has made various helpful suggestions.

Fletcher distinguishes four types of euthanasia that derive their importance from the fact that the "incompetent" condition of many of the dying makes voluntary, patient-chosen euthanasia a minority type of elective death.

(1)   *Voluntary and direct euthanasia* occurs where the death is chosen and carried out by the patient, e.g., an overdose is left near at hand. Fletcher (1973, p. 117) concedes that this is a form of suicide.

(2)   *Voluntary but indirect euthanasia* occurs where the patient gives to others the discretion to end his life when the situation requires, if the patient becomes too comatose or dysfunctioned to make the decision *pro forma*, e.g., exacting a promise that if the overdose cannot be self-administered somebody will do it for the patient.

(3)   *Direct but involuntary euthanasia* occurs where a simple "mercy killing" is done on a patient's behalf without his present or past request, e.g., the death of a child in the worst stages of Tay-Sachs disease is speeded up, or a shutdown is ordered on a patient in a deeply mindless condition.

(4)   *Indirect and involuntary euthanasia* occurs where a "letting-go" of the patient takes place: "Nothing is done for the patient positively to release him from his tragic condition (other than "trying to make him comfortable") and what is done negatively is decided *for* him rather than in response to his request" (Fletcher, 1973, p. 118).

Before evaluating Fletcher's proposal, it is well to note that the distinction between active and passive euthanasia, defined after the fashion of chapter VIII, will be incorporated into the vocabulary of

4. Fletcher (1973, p. 113) observes that passive euthanasia is a fait accompli in modern hospital practice.

5. See Freeman (1972).

the typology.[6] Although Fletcher himself may not accept such a distinction, we will carry it over in our treatment as a part of the taxonomy we have developed here.

In addition, we need also to assume that we know what is meant by saying that an action is *voluntary*. It takes us too far afield to dwell on this protean notion, so we must simply allow Fletcher his assumption that it has some clear meaning for us, and that it is a useful category in the study of euthanasia. A suggestive discussion of voluntariness in the law is found in Hart and Honoré (1969), and an attempt to characterize a related concept of "control" that may also be of some assistance is found in Walton (1974).

We now turn to the question of what sort of underlying direct-indirect distinction is operative in Fletcher's quadratic typology of euthanasia. The voluntary aspect is clear enough as far as the basic idea is concerned: voluntary euthanasia is death specifically requested or chosen by the patient himself even if he does not carry out the "act" himself. But the indirect aspect appears a little harder to grasp clearly. It might seem characteristic of indirect euthanasia that the "act" is carried out by another agent, but (3) quite clearly rules out this suggestion. On what basis then is the decision made that (1) and (3) are direct whereas (2) and (4) are indirect? Fletcher gives no specific guidance on this question at all. Intuitively the distinction between the two pairs would seem to be as follows. (1) and (3) are "direct" because once the agent has made his decision, he is able to follow it through at the time he wishes, even immediately if the necessary conditions are present. In the case of (2), by contrast, this element of immediacy is lacking—once the decision is made there may be an indefinite interval before it is executed, and the agent is not able to follow through at a specific time of his choosing. (2) also seems "indirect" because there is a conventional R-relation involved, unlike the cases (1) and (3). In (4) however, there is no conventional R-relation apparent, but (4) does seem "indirect" in the sense that the agent, once he has decided to act, cannot follow through at a specific time of his choosing. Why not? The only plausible reason I find is that an omission is more difficult to date specifically than a positive action, and in addition, an omission of

6. *Active euthanasia* has the form "*a* brings it about that *b* is dead" and *passive euthanasia* has the form "*a* does not bring it about that *b* is not dead" (*a* allows *b* to die). Their relation is like that between the universal and existential quantifiers, according to the account given in chapters VII and VIII.

the kind thought of here would likely take place over an extended period of time. Thus the difficulty I have with Fletcher's classification is that (4) seems indistinguishable from the case of passive euthanasia and consequently does not seem to belong in the fourfold typology at all, being rather an instance of a quite different, but equally relevant distinction. Also, since there is some question about exactly what "indirect" means in relation to (2), whether there can be a legitimate and significant instance of euthanasia of kind (4) is unclear and appears dubious. Clearly these are more problems of statement than of the general thrust of the typology. Therefore let us see if we can preserve the intent of the classification while ameliorating these specific difficulties.

Kinds of Euthanasia

In my view, Fletcher's analysis does indicate the importance of a set of four pairs of distinctions that do need to be applied to euthanasia: *active* and *passive* euthanasia, *personal* and *interpersonal* euthanasia, *voluntary* and *involuntary* euthanasia,[7] *direct* and *indirect* euthanasia. But the logic of combining these distinctions needs to be more refined than a simple pairing of the various permutations in order to remove the problems and at the same time make the typology more generally applicable. We will briefly sketch a basis of this logic to provide some foundations for extending Fletcher's work.

First, we should note that indirectness can be a relative matter, e.g., suppose A stands in an R-relation to B and B stands in the same R-relation to C. Then if a brings about A, he R-indirectly brings about B and also R-indirectly brings about C, but his bringing about C is more indirect than his bringing about B. In other words, there are levels of indirectness. If I ignite a gas-soaked rag and burn down the house, igniting the rag is level-one indirect in relation to making a certain motion with a match, but the burning of the house is level-two indirect in relation to the level-zero event of the motion of the match.[8] Thus even though (1) and (3) are perhaps indirect actions in some sense, (2) is intuitively indirect with greater force because it seems *more indirect*.

7. Some may feel however that *all* legitimate cases of what is properly called euthanasia must be voluntary, e.g. Kohl (1973).
8. See the discussions in Davidson (1971) and Walton (1976c).

Second, since omissions as well as positive actions can be combined with *R*-relations to yield action, "*a* brings about *A* and *A* stands in an *R*-relation to *B*" will have variants like "*a* does not bring about *A* and not-*A* stands in an *R*-relation to *B*." Also we will have cases of passive indirect action: "*a* does not bring about not-*A* and *A* stands in an *R*-relation to *B*." We can construct interesting variants of these kinds of expressions, but we will leave this exercise to the next chapter, having at least now indicated the motivation for further developments. We should also reiterate that correctly characterizing an omission, as opposed to a mere not-bringing-about, involves a notion of control or "voluntariness." It is correct to say that I do not move a certain grain of sand in the middle of the Sahara today quite independently of the question of my control over such an event, but it is only correct to say that I omitted to wear a lifejacket while out boating yesterday if I had control over whether or not I was to wear a lifejacket. In short, not doing *A* is not always omitting to do *A*, in the strong sense of "omitting" that might pertain to culpability.[9]

Third, interpersonal actions can be combined with indirect actions. If *a* brings it about that *A* and *A* stands in an *R*-relation to *b*'s bringing it about that *B*, then there is a sense in which *a* brings it about that *b* brings it about that *B*.[10] In these cases, it becomes quite a complicated matter indeed to unravel questions of moral or legal responsibility, and the criminal law is replete with cases of inter-personal transactions that exhibit interesting action-theoretic structure as indicated by Hart and Honoré (1969). Fletcher's case (2) is of this general type, a type that is of paramount critical importance for our understanding of the meaning of euthanasia. These cases are complicated by the fact that various different kinds of *R*-relations are relevant, and the *R*-relations differ in their varying tendencies to affect the moral-legal question of the withdrawal or distribution of responsibility for the joint action.

Principles of Action

Obviously much work remains to be done in (i) further studying the formalities of this fragment of the logic of action and (ii) applying it

9. See Åqvist (1974) and Hart and Honoré (1969).
10. The reader should now be in a position to formulate various other interesting varieties of elective death, e.g., *passive indirect interpersonal euthanasia* has the structure: *a* does not bring it about that *A* does not occur and *A* stands in an *R*-relation to *b*'s bringing it about that *B* occurs (where *B* is the death of *a*).

to problems of practice; but perhaps enough has been said now to indicate that the structure of Fletcher-type typologies is an interesting object of study as an adjunct to multidisciplinary work on euthanasia. I think the most important aspect of the above analysis, in connection with the direction of future work, is the revelation that general principles of human action underlie Fletcher's typologies. The practical problems of medical ethics are an application of, and to a certain extent a testing-ground for, philosophical theories of human action. The connection between logical theory and actual practice is of course mediated by a multiplicity of intermediate levels of inquiry—analytical analysis of concepts of action will not in itself yield ready answers to the life-or-death dilemmas of medical ethics. What it will give us is a vocabulary based in logic for intelligently asking the right questions in the right form, and the necessary ability to distinguish clearly between confused and unclear questions based in obscure language. Logical action theory alone will not yield up a decision procedure to tell us that active euthanasia is bad but passive euthanasia is permissible in a given real-life case. There are clearly substantive moral decisions involved at the practical level.[11] But action theory may suggest clear and logically adequate means of distinguishing between active and passive euthanasia at a conceptual level so that we are in a position at least to investigate consistently the ethical question of whether both kinds of action are always equally morally assessible, or whether there is some intrinsic difference in the mode of moral evaluation appropriate to each. Similar ethical questions about voluntary versus involuntary euthanasia, direct and indirect euthanasia, personal and interpersonal euthanasia, can now

11. A physician has pointed out to me that a fuller description of the context of the termination of life reveals some interesting moral complexities. Often there might be two decision points. First, the physician has to decide whether to bring in resuscitative procedures without definite knowledge of a patient's future capabilities. He might die, he might completely recover, or he might be permanently damaged yet live. If the third possibility occurs, then a second decision point may be reached where the familiar moral dilemma of removing the ventilator is posed. But if we reflect back to the first point, a secondary moral dilemma may be generated. Unlike the situation at the second point, back at the first point it may not have been clear that death was inevitable at the time the decision to resuscitate was made. So there would seem less risk of the doctor's being morally wrong by withholding resuscitation shortly after the time of injury than at the second point, where he considers removing the ventilator from the patient with proven brain death. Yet it is clear that it would be wrong for the doctor not to resuscitate at the first point if recovery is possible.

at least be posed in a climate that is at least not theoretically totally unregulated and open to any interpretations the questioner might wish.

Chapter X

Bringing-About, Allowing, and Action Chains

The basic distinction we sought in chapters VII and VIII turned essentially on the logical notion of *negation*, and the principles we attempted to clarify in chapter IX additionally involved the key notion of the *conditional* in action contexts. Both chapters therefore suggest that if we are to have a clear foundation basis in theory for beginning to understand how to work with the needed action concepts, we must turn to the general question of the logic of bringing-about specifically in the area of negation and conditionals. So far, we have been grappling with bringing-about, negation, and conditionals in a rather practical way, involved as we are in certain substantive ethical controversies, but I think that we are now in a position to see that if the distinctions unearthed in the three preceding chapters are to be adequately perspicuous at the theoretical level, we must ascend to a general discussion of the language of action. Some readers will undoubtedly have little patience with or interest in the "theoretical niceties" that follow and regard them as redundant. Others will surely lament the lack of further logical analysis and regard the theory developed here as a mere preliminary light exercise in heuristics. However, any attempt of the type we are engaging in to bring theory and practice towards some common meeting ground is open to the simultaneously contradictory criticisms of being at once too theoretical and too practical. The best we can hope for is to go far enough in either direction to open up the lines of communication and dialogue. In this quest, we extend our study of the logic of action somewhat further in the direction of theory, trying along the way to show how we can enrich the capacity of the theory in various directions, consolidate it to deal with some major criticisms, and chart the limits of its expressive capabilities. None of these objectives will be carried out in the exact method characteristic of formal analysis and logic. But we are hoping that looking at bringing-about, negation, and conditionals within a minimal, basic framework that can be exclusively characterized by elementary set theory, will at least sharpen the foundational basis of the distinctions we seek in a way that might encourage others to continue more exact methods of analysis. We ought now to appreciate that the notion of "bringing-about" that is at the bottom of our varied concerns is (a) fundamental, in the sense of being a powerful primitive notion in all practical thinking; (b) a very vague, indeed slippery notion; and (c) possibly, and indeed almost certainly, highly ambiguous. Therefore the advantages of a move in the direction of precision of statement, even if it leads to the theoretical, are not to be dismissed too easily.

Action Chains

There is an understandable proclivity to think initially of an "action" as a more or less discrete, unified event that takes place in a fairly narrow and well-defined spatio-temporal region. An "action," for example, is often identified with a single bodily movement, e.g., a specific occasion of my moving my finger. Our discussion in previous chapters, especially chapter IX, showed us, however, that actions can often be "spread out" over conditionals, forming what we called "action chains" or "accordions." To reiterate the familiar example: I move my finger, flicking the switch, turning the light on, warning a prowler.[1] By bringing it about that my finger moves, I bring it about that something happens later, namely that a prowler is warned. Thus bringing-about is carried forward over a set of conditions to form an action chain. Similarly, I pull a trigger and as a result someone later dies of a gunshot wound. Here the action of "killing" is not adequately identified with one specific, discrete event that took place at a specific point or short stretch of time but needs to be understood as a chain of events. Actions have a way of carrying themselves forward in time towards the future over consequences. How can we understand how bringing-about is preserved over

1. See Davidson (1966 and 1971) and Walton (1976b). Useful background material is found in Brand (1970) and Brand and Walton (1976).

conditionals where temporal intervals are involved?[2] In other words, how can we extend the notion of bringing-about outlined in chapter VIII to contend with the action chains that so obviously played the key role in chapter IX?

In phrasing the question this way, we are introducing an important limitation into the scope of our inquiry. For in studying the properties of bringing-about over action chains, our primary concern will be to see how bringing-about is preserved over action chains. To put it somewhat roughly, our concern will be to see how actions are carried forward temporally over chains rather than to see how the action entered into the chain in the first place. Though the latter phenomenon will be shown to be also relevant to our concerns, our theory will at least initially be directed towards modelling the first phenomenon. As David Hume,[3] and many philosophers both before and since Hume have noticed, in action or causal language there is mixed an element of necessity and observation. The problems of action and causation often seem to turn on how observation (i.e., in the case of action, observable bodily movements, or behavior) is connected with the "logical" element of necessity that ties the behavior to its result.[4] Since the factors pertaining to bodily movements and actual episodes of behavior are obviously strongly empirical (more in the area of psychology or other social sciences), and the factors pertaining to the element of necessity are more oriented to logic and abstract conceptual analysis, obviously it makes sense for us to concentrate on the latter area if we expect logical, analytical methods to the most appropriate. So to a certain extent, we shall bypass "action" in the broader sense, and concentrate on the areas where bringing-about intersects with negation and conditionals, these being (a) appropriate targets of logical analysis, and (b) at the heart of our difficulties with "omissions," "allowing" and "chains." Just as it is often said that logic does not give a general decision procedure for the truth of the premiss-set of any argument but is more narrowly concerned with certain kinds of relations (implication,

2. See also my paper "Time and Modality in the *Can* of Opportunity" in Brand and Walton (1976, pp. 271–88).

3. David Hume, *A Treatise of Human Nature*, ed. L. A. Selby-Bigge (Oxford: The Clarendon Press, 1888), Book I, Part III.

4. Davidson (1971) is particularly good on this aspect of actions. See also Donald Davidson, "Causal Relations," *Journal of Philosophy*, LXIV (1967): 691–703.

consistency, etc.) among premisses and conclusions, so we will not expect our logical analysis of actions to tell us whether an actual episode of behavior has or has not occurred, but only whether certain relations obtain among such possible episodes.

Possible-Outcome Trees and Inevitability

We start by postulating a set of "hypothetical situations" or "possible worlds," $W_1, W_2, \ldots, W_k$. We are thinking of these worlds in such a manner that some worlds are possible causal outcomes of others, i.e., relative to a given state of a world at a time there are various possible alternative outcomes that might develop.

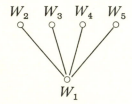

The sort of relationship between W_1 and the set $\{W_2, W_3, W_4, W_5\}$ we have in mind is that W_1 *can cause* W_2 or W_3 or W_4,[5] i.e., the modality is that of possibility. We are not thinking of the relation W_1 *does cause* W_2 etc. Thus the nodes represent possible situations and the lines joining the nodes can be thought of as representing a relation, $<$.[6] We are thinking of this relation among the possible situations in such a way that two given possible situations W_j and W_k are only thought of as possible outcomes relative to a given world, W_i. That is, we can never have "converging worlds" as on the left, but only "diverging worlds," as on the right.

5. For a much more theoretically oriented discussion of this notion, see George Berger, "Temporally Symmetric Causal Relations in Minkowski Space-Time," in Patrick Suppes (ed.), *Space, Time and Geometry* (Dordrecht: Reidel, 1973), pp. 56–71.
6. We are thinking of the relation $<$ as irreflexive, anti-symmetric and transitive.

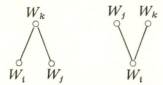

Intuitively, we are thinking of the possible worlds as "opening" towards the future (to the top of the page) and "closing" towards the past (to the bottom of the page). In other words, two worlds can only be identical if they share a unique past. So we are thinking of the possible worlds as possible developments of a world in time (towards the future).

Time is often thought of as linear,[7] but since we are concerned with alternative possible developments of a situation, we will think of time as branching. Accordingly, we lay down the following condition on our ordering $<$ of the worlds: for any worlds W_i, W_j, W_k, if $W_i < W_k$ and $W_j < W_k$ then $W_i < W_j$ or $W_j < W_i$ if $W_i \neq W_j$.[8] This condition simply rules out the situation on the left. If two worlds W_i and W_j precede a given world W_k then unless W_i and W_j are the same world, one must precede the other. In other words, we will not allow "loops"

to occur.[9] The worlds will only branch towards the future. The resultant ordering of worlds by $<$ will in general take the form of a "tree,"[10] e.g.,

7. See Prior (1967).

8. The framework here is thus similar to that of Thomason (1970). A somewhat different way of defining the same type of structure is given in Åqvist (1974) and Kripke (1963). Readers who wish a more formal treatment are directed to these sources.

9. We could allow loops to occur. Then the resulting structure would be similar to a "causal net." See the discussion in Bas von Fraassen, *An Introduction to the Philosophy of Space and Time* (New York: Random House, 1970), pp. 173ff.

10. The centrality of "tree" structures in the causal analysis of action is brought out very clearly and revealingly in Von Wright (1968) and also in more recent works of Von Wright.

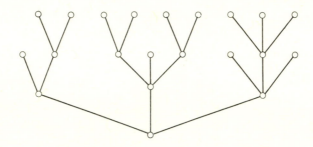

Next, we need to introduce the notion of a *path* through a tree. A path is just a linear subset of the set of nodes of the tree. For example, the set of darkened dots would constitute a path on the tree below.

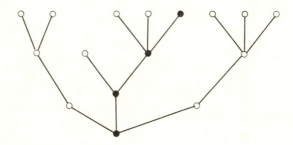

We lay down as the defining condition for a path that it be a subset of the set of points on a tree that is linear, i.e., for any two points W_i and W_j, if $W_i \neq W_j$ then $W_i < W_j$ or $W_j < W_i$.[11] In other words on a path, no branching in either direction is allowed—one point must always either precede, or be preceded by, another. No "adjacent" points are allowed. The path on the tree above is also a *maximal path*, i.e., it is the largest subset. In other words, a maximal path is simply a path that is as long (in both directions) as it can possibly be, given the "length" of the tree. Now we introduce the idea of a *possible future* of a world W_i: this simply refers to the maximal path beyond W_i. For example, in the tree below, there are three possible futures of W_i, each indicated by an enclosed area.

11. See also Thomason (1970, p. 267).

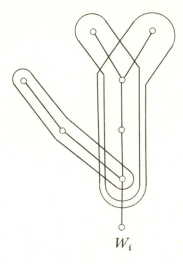

W_i

Next we introduce the idea that a proposition, p, q, r, ... can be true at (or in) a possible world.[12] Given that we can talk this way, we can easily introduce the idea that a proposition p is *inevitable* at a given world W_i in the sense of being true in all possible futures of W_i. We do this through the following definition: *p is inevitable at W_i if, and only if, p is true in at least one world on every maximal path beyond W_i.*[13] Thus p is said to be "inevitable" in relation to a given world W_i in that no matter what path we take along a path leading from W_i on a tree, we must "bump into" p-p is "unavoidable."

It might be clearer to add that we are thinking of *inevitability at some time or other*, i.e., p is said to be inevitable at W_i if at some world or other preceded by W_i you will arrive at the truth of p. Thus to say that p is inevitable in this sense does not mean that p will obtain at a specific time, but only that, the possibilities being what they are, p will become realized at some time or other. On the diagram on page 140 p is true at W_4, W_5, and W_6, and it is not the case that p is true at any of the other points.

12. This way of speaking derives from the tradition set by Kripke (1963) and is clearly explained in the context of logic by Hughes and Cresswell (1968).

13. This is a reformulation of the notion of Thomason (1970).

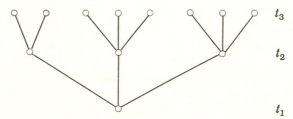

Then, for example, p is inevitable at W_2, but it is not the case that p is inevitable at W_0. Finally, we should note that we could define "inevitability at a time," and various related notions, by introducing a ranking of levels of nodes of a tree[14] as suggested by the following example.

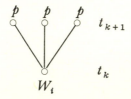

Thus we could speak of the inevitability of p at a world W_i at t_k at the next time t_{k+1}.

To describe this situation we might say that p is *directly inevitable* at W_i (or "inevitable at the next moment" or something of the sort).

14. This method is explicitly carried out in a rather rigorous fashion in Åqvist (1974). In general, the structure outlined here bears some important resemblances to that of Åqvist (1974) but Åqvist's theory is technically much more developed and also quite different in critical points of methodology and objectives. Some discussion and explication of Åqvist's theory is found in Walton (1977).

Negation and Conditionals in Tree Structures

As we said earlier, a set of propositions, p, q, r, . . . can be thought of as mapped into the points W_1, W_2, . . . such that p may be said to be true at some points. Additionally, propositions of the form $\neg p$ (not-p) may also be true at some points. Here the rule is: p is true at a point, W_i, exactly where $\neg p$ is not true at W_i (ie., $\neg$ is classical negation). Next we take the step of equating $I_{p_{w_i}}$ with the reading "p is (strategically) brought about by some agent at W_i." Accordingly, we can now define a number of interesting ideas.

(a) $\neg I_{p_{w_i}}$: it is not the case that p is (strategically) brought about (by some agent) at W_i: p is not-true in some possible future of W_i (i.e., it is not the case that p is true in all possible futures of W_i).

(b) $I \neg_{p_{w_i}}$: not-p is (strategically) brought about (by some agent) at W_i: p is not-true in every possible future of W_i.

(c) $\neg I \neg p_{w_i}$: it is not the case that not-p is (strategically) brought about by some agent at W_i: p is true in some possible future of W_i (i.e., it is not the case that (b)).

Now we can introduce the expression $A_{p_{w_i}}$ (p is allowed by some agent at W_i; some agent at W_i lets p be true) as a short form for $\neg I \neg p_{w_i}$.

So far, we have introduced negation. We could also introduce a type of conditional, $p \to q$: at every world at which p is true, q is inevitable. It is now easy to see that the following will be generally true: If $I_{p_{w_i}}$ and $p \to q$, then $I_{q_{w_i}}$. That is: if p is inevitable at a point W_i and q is true in every possible future of W_i in which p is true, then q will be true in every possible future of W_i too.

To a certain extent, the language of I, $\neg$, and $\to$ may enable us to see how "action" can be preserved over "action chains" and thus throw some light on our problems related to actions in the context of negation and conditionals. We can see how if we reflect on some problems pertaining to the expression, "The agent a brought about q at t_2 by bringing about p at t_1."

Some Limitations of the Language

Our equation of "a brings it about that p" with $\ulcorner I_p \urcorner$ is wider than the notion of bringing-about apparently presupposed by Rachels or

Tooley,[15] since by our equation, Smith and Jones both brought about the deaths of their respective cousins.[16] In another way, however, the equation results in a notion of bringing-about that is too wide. To see how, consider the third case of Robinson, who is in Singapore on business while his young cousin, whom he has never met or even seen, drowns in a bathtub in Portage La Prairie. If we assume that it is "inevitable" that the cousin drowned at that time, then we must assume that some agent (Robinson?) brought it about that the cousin died. Clearly, in other words, there is a difference between "inevitability" and bringing-about by an agent. And consequently, in order to have a very realistic theory of bringing-about, we will have to set down some restrictions on the notion of "inevitability" so far defined.[17] One suggestion for doing this runs as follows. Let us think of a given world W_i as an *entry point* on an action chain. Roughly put, the idea is this: an entry point is one point where bodily movements can enter into or fail to enter into an action chain. The limitations of the theory are, again very roughly, that it does not enable us to decide whether a bodily movement of an agent does in fact enter nor whether a bodily movement can enter or not. The theory only tells us how actions are transmitted over action chains, i.e., once we are "on" the chain, the theory explains how "bringing-about" is carried forward over the chain. These limitations will be reflected in the theory's capabilities in dealing with the following five problems.

1. *The Leaky Rowboat*: (Foot, 1967, p. 270) " . . . it is possible to *bring about* a man's death by getting him to go to sea in a leaky boat. . . . " Here we would seem to have a case of "strategic bringing about," except that *two* agents may be involved. Can one agent "bring it about" that another agent brings something about?

2. *The Drowned Cousin* (Rachels): in both the cases of Smith and Jones, the death of the cousin is *brought about* (strategically) rather than merely allowed, according to our theory. But why is one case thought to be an omission (by Rachels and Tooley) and the other not? Contrast these two cases with that of Robinson, who holds a

15. See Rachels (1975), and Tooley (1972 and 1976).
16. This point may not be obvious, but a little reflection should show its plausibility.
17. Similar moves are adopted by Pörn (1974) and Åqvist (1974). I have tried to indicate some problems with their methods in Walton (1977).

board over the tub to make sure his cousin drowns. Does what Robinson did constitute "bringing-about" or is it a mere "letting-happen" in some sense?

3. *The President and the Rocket*: for a ceremonial rocket firing, the engineer has rigged up a circuit such that if the president pushes a button at time zero, he will activate the circuit that fires the rocket. But the engineer has set it up so that, if the president "bumbles" and fails to push the button at t_0, the rocket will be fired anyway. That is there are two circuits—if the president's circuit is activated at the right time, it will cut out the other circuit.

Engineer's Circuit   o—o—o—o—o—o—o—o—o   Rocket

President's Circuit   o—o—o—o—o—o

Who "brought about" the firing of the rocket? This case was brought to my attention by David Lewis, in discussion.

4. *Doubly Doomed Jones*: Smith pushes Jones off the thirtieth floor of a building, having removed some intervening balconies previously, i.e., Smith brings it about that Jones is dead. But Schmidt fatally and instantaneously atomizes Jones by hitting him with a bazooka projectile just as Jones hits the pavement. Who "brought about" Jones' death?

5. *The Water Bottle*: Jones is preparing an expedition into the desert where he would certainly die of thirst without his canteen of water. Smith poisons the water. But then Schmidt (not knowing about the poison) empties the canteen. Who "brought about" Jones' death?

Up until now, we have allowed ourselves the convenient if simplistic assumption that the agent is alone in nature. But clearly if our theory is to clarify the sort of distinctions it seeks to, we will have to extend it to two-person and many-person cases.[18] We will begin to do this in an elementary way in the section, Kinds of Letting-Happen. For the time being, the theory rules that the person who got the other to go to sea in the leaky boat brought about the death of his victim if and only if relative to the given situation at the time, the

18. The methods of Åqvist (1974) are useful here.

sinking of the boat with its fatal consequences was a possible outcome that obtained in every possible future relative to the possible
bodily movements of the agent. In other words if there was a
possible future in which the person in the boat decided not to set out
to sea, then the other agent did not "bring about" his demise in the
fullest sense of this term. The critical factor is the notion of inevitability. Obviously however, a fuller description of the interpersonal
relationship between the two agents here may make the application
of this criterion problematic. The reader is referred to Hart and
Honoré (1969) for various interesting cases of this type.[19]

Case 2 also brings out an important limitation of our theory of
bringing-about. It may seem that the cases of Smith and Jones in
connection with the "drowned cousin" reflects an important distinction between bringing-about and letting-happen because, in the
one case, but not the other, bodily movements were (directly)
involved in the outcome. Our theory does not tell us, of course,
whether there is an actual bodily movement on an action chain. But
if we can empirically identify bodily movements in a clear way, we
could add, after the fashion of Davidson (1971), a concept "bodily
movement" to the theory in order to extend it in this direction.
Toward this end, we have recognized the notion of an *entry point* on an
action chain. But the question of how bodily movements enter into
action chains is rather complex. For example, Robinson exhibited a
bodily movement too, but he did not directly bring about the death
of his cousin in quite the same direct "causal" way that the first
agent did (by reaching our and pushing the child's head under).[20]
Clearly therefore, much more work needs to be done on the problem
of how bodily movements "enter into" action chains. I mentioned
before that we could perhaps avoid the nettlesome question of "basic
actions" in exploring this type of problem, even if one authority
(Davidson, 1971) identifies bodily movements with basic actions.

The "President and the Rocket" is a genuine, and I think, a
rather deep puzzle for us. The best we can do here is to say that in
our sense of strategic bringing-about (ensuring, making inevitable),
the engineer, and not the president, is the one who brings about the
firing of the rocket. Obviously, however, there is a sense in which the
president "brought it about" too—his bodily movement was the

19. The discussion in Walton (1974) of "joint control" is relevant to these
problems. See also Rescher (1969).
20. I owe this important observation to Risto Hilpinen.

actual "imminent" cause. Thus our theory of bringing-about simply does not seem to capture the essential "pushiness" of actual agency. In the section, Direct Actions, however, we will show how it can be extended some way in this direction.

Cases 4 and 5 reflect similar puzzles. There seems to be dichotomy between "strategic bringing-about" and "actual bringing-about." However, in Kinds of Letting-Happen, we will try to show how our theory can be brought to bear on some cases rather like these that are very important for medical ethics. In the meantime, it is well to be aware that our theory is incomplete in its capacity to deal with various important aspects of cases 1 to 5.

Thomson Problems

Suppose a shoots b, and b staggers off and eventually dies (say a few hours, or even days, later). When did a kill b? At the time the trigger was pulled? No—because b was still alive then. At the time the bullet entered b's body? No—again, b was presumably still alive then. What about the time at which b (later) expired? This does not seem quite right either, since we often speak in such a way as to imply that the time (or place) of the killing is in the spatio-temporal vicinity of the shooting. A witness might say that he saw the killing if he only saw the shooting episode. When is the right time? There does seem to be a sense, Thomson notes, in which one might say that a has "killed" b once the bullet has entered b's body if the wound is truly fatal. But this must be a peculiar sense of "kill" because, at that time, b is *still alive*, even though it may be a certainty that he will shortly die. Thomson calls this the *Hollywood use of language*, e.g., "Sometimes in the movies, the villain shoots one of his underlings, who looks up shocked, and says 'You killed me, Big Al!' But note that sometimes also the villain says *before* he shoots, 'You're, dead, Little Joe; you don't know it yet, but you are,' and surely that can't have been true" (Thomson, 1971, p. 120). Our theory can help to explain why we are systematically confused about the time of the killing. Since we think of the killing naively as a simple event, an action, we think that it should take place at one single time. But our theory can show that more than one time is involved, and how the times are related. Take the situation at W_i, the entry point, to be the bodily movement involved in pulling the trigger. Then relative to the situation at that time, a certain outcome p, the death of b, was inevitable at some time or other. In other words, we have two sets of times: the unit set $\{W_i\}$ and the set of worlds $\{W_j, W_k, \ldots\}$ at which p is true. Accordingly, we think of the action in a binary way: first, we have an initial time, or entry-point, and second, a set of possible-outcome-times. Thus there is no single "time of the action." Rather there is one time at which the action was "set into motion," and a set of times at which the action must successfully be culminated. Once b does in fact die, then one of the second set will be a unique actual time at which the death of b did actually occur. This makes things even more confusing because, according to this (hindsight) view of the matter, there are two definite times of initiation and culmination respectively. Thus it matters whether we are thinking of the action from a viewpoint of someone looking towards the future (as nicely suggested by our branching "trees"), or from the viewpoint of someone looking back to a completed action in the past. All this can lead to many basic confusions, and our theory helps us to better understand the basic structure of action chains.

The Problematic Types of Cases in Medical Ethics

Now we should address ourselves to the controversial cases of medical ethics where the physician is thought to have, in some sense, allowed death to occur rather than to have (actively) brought it about. First we need to note that our account of bringing-about allows for two distinctions that might correspond to the sort of distinction that is relevant to medical ethics: (1) At the "entry point," W_i, we can have a bodily movement or an "omission," i.e., a possibly bodily movement that could have entered into the action chain but did not. The distinction here turns on whether there was an actual bodily movement involved or not. (2) p is *brought about* if p is true on all possible futures of W_i, but p is merely *allowed* if p is true on some possible future of W_i. Let us consider two particularly controversial types of cases: (a) The patient is unquestionably in a terminal state and shortly about to die, and the medical team decides, on grounds of alleviation of great suffering, not to bring in the use of emergency resuscitation devices. (b) The patient is on a ventilator but unquestionably in a terminal state and about to die shortly, and the medical team decides to discontinue therapy (e.g., "pull the plug"). Now it is quite clear that, as far as bodily movements are concerned, we have some in (b) but we need not have any, at least of the same kind, in (a). Thus (a), but, not (b), can qualify as "allowing" according to distinction (1).[21] But how do we stand in regard to (2)? Take case (b) first. Here we may say that death is "inevitable" over a certain range of times $\mathscr{R}$ (sometime fairly soon, let us postulate), relative to a situation W_i in which no action is taken. But death is also "inevitable" over a less remote range of times $\mathscr{R}\text{-}\Delta$ relative to an "entry point' v_i in which certain bodily movements do actually occur (the plug is pulled).

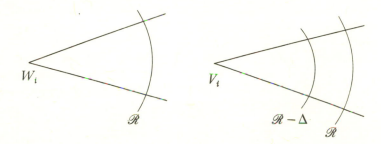

How would this justify our ruling that given the situation on the left, the situation on the right constitutes only a "letting-happen" rather than a "making-happen." In other words, how is it that the situation represented on the right is such that p is true in some but not all possible futures of V_i? In attempting to answer, first we need to note that the inevitability of p at W_i does not merely by itself undercut or reduce the inevitability of p at V_i even if the time difference Δ is relatively short. Surely "speeding up" the death of an individual, even if he is inevitably about to die shortly anyway, is to bring about his death and not merely to "allow" him to die. So the mere fact that p is already inevitable should not by itself constitute adequate grounds for concluding that bringing p about sooner is only to make p true in some but not all possible futures relative to the given situation. At least if such a reduction is to be justified, it will take further steps to show clearly how it is to be done along these lines.

21. One might try to argue that (b) was a mere allowing on the basis that discontinuation of therapy is an instance of "not-doing" in the sense of "undoing something that was previously done." But consider a parallel case: I take away your gas mask that I have previously given you. As a result, you die. Surely I brought about your death.

So we will at least provisionally reject the answer that the inevitability at W_i is alone sufficient to warrant a conclusion of "allowing."

The most natural response would seem to entail splitting (b) into two cases: (b1) Pulling the plug directly and inevitably brings about death. (b2) If the plug is pulled the patient has a reasonable chance of surviving as long as he otherwise might, but the possibility is introduced that he may die sooner. Both (b1) and (b2) correspond to some kinds of cases that have been discussed in the area of medical ethics of euthanasia. It would be (b2) that could be reconstructed as an "allowing" within our framework of bringing-about, as follows. There is a certain range or time-zone (set of points) $\mathcal{R}$ at which p (the death of the patient) is inevitable relative to a world W_i, and another range $\mathcal{R}'$ relative to V_i. The physician allows (but doesn't bring it about that) p exactly where $\mathcal{R}$ and $\mathcal{R}'$ overlap. The idea is that some points are relative to W_i, not *all* to V_i.

An example would be as follows. In the situation represented on the left the patient must die within the range $\mathcal{R}$ of possible times pictured in the enclosed space.

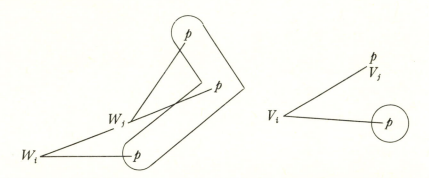

By "pulling the plug" the range $\mathcal{R}$ is restricted to the smaller range consisting of the two points on the right, i.e., the situation with respect to p was "still open" at W_j, but is closed at V_j. But in this case notice that one point at which p is true in relation to V_i (circled at right), is analogous to a point that already comes within $\mathcal{R}$ on the left, i.e., $\{p\}$ on the right is a subset of the set of point $\mathcal{R}$ on the left.[22]

22. The idea is this: if we transpose the diagram on the right (assuming it to be inscribed on clear plastic) over the diagram on the left, there will be at least one point where a p will fit over another p at the same point (in this case the lowest point).

What this represents is that the agent, in shifting the situation from left to right by his action, only made it possible (allowed) that p because p, so to speak, was already true at one point. That is, we look at the possibilities from the point of view of the situation at V_i. One of two things could be a possible outcome. But one possible outcome, the circled one, was already established. Thus the agent's making it true that p at V_j only constitutes an allowing or making-it-possible that p.

Kinds of Letting-Happen

Generally, p is allowed, rather than brought about if, and only if, p is true in all possible futures of an entry point V_i at a given set of points $\mathscr{R}$, but relative to another point W_i (which can represent either "natural inevitability," as above, or an entry point of a second agent) p is true in all possible futures at a set of points $\mathscr{R}'$, and (i) $\mathscr{R} \cap \mathscr{R}' \neq \varnothing$, (ii) $\mathscr{R} - \mathscr{R}' \neq \varnothing$, and (iii) $\mathscr{R}' - \mathscr{R} \neq \varnothing$. This general characterization can be explained more clearly as follows. What we are suggesting is that there may be two possible entry points relative to a given state of the world at a time such that a given outcome p is inevitable relative to each point taken by itself. But since we are taking each entry point as representing a possible outcome of the same given stage of some actual train of events, at least in a real-life application, we need to compare both sets of possible outcomes. Let us say that we do compare them by transposing one over the other. Each set of possible outcomes will have a subset representing the set of all points at which p is true. Now it is exactly where these subsets overlap that we have a case of allowing. Take V_i as the entry point for a possible bodily movement of agent a, and W_i for agent b. One of these "agents" can be Nature if we like. Considered apart, we have in each case, let us say, a bringing-about of p over a certain perhaps not very well-defined range of times represented below by an enclosed area.

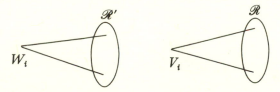

Now it is just in the case where these areas overlap that we have an allowing in the case of each party where both actions are considered together.

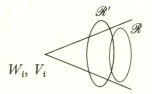

Also, it is easy to see that we have a "double allowing" only where the complement of each set in non-null. If $\mathscr{R}' \subset \mathscr{R}$ then a's action at V_i must be ruled a bringing-about and not merely an allowing of p. Similarly, if $\mathscr{R} \subset \mathscr{R}'$ then b's action at W_i is a bringing-about rather than a letting-happen. That is why we rule in the general account that for there to be a genuine two-way allowing, there must be genuine overlap of possible outcomes rather than absorption of one set of outcomes into the other.

We have now, in effect, drawn a distinction between two kinds of "allowing" even within category (2) above: (2a) the agent allows p to happen in the sense that p is true in some possible future of an entry point for that agent, (2b) an agent jointly brings it about that p with some other agent (or Nature, which might be described here as a kind of pseudo-agent) in such a fashion that, given a characteristic point-range overlap of sets of worlds in which p is true as described above, each agent may be said to have merely "allowed" p to obtain. The distinction may be highlighted by observing that an entailment like the following is true of (2b), but not necessarily true in a case of (2a): "a allows that p" entails p. Sanford (1976, p. 4) postulates that "X let Y die" entails "Y died," and suggests that an analysis of Dinello (1971) is incorrect insofar as it does not preserve this entailment. Our analysis, in bringing out yet another ambiguity implicit in the language of letting-happen, shows that whether or not the entailment holds may depend on what sort of "allowing" one has in mind. Perhaps some verbal distinctions between "allowing," "letting-happen," "making possible," might help us here. I would suggest that to cover the case of (2a), we might use a phrase like "a makes it possible that p" or "a let it might be that p," whereas for (2b) "a let it be that p" or "a allowed p" is more strictly appropriate.

Direct Actions

We can now see how the theory of chapter X is an extension of that of chapter VIII, even if many details of the relationship remain to be filled in. In chapter VIII, we thought of only "one-step" sets of possible outcomes whereas in chapter X we generalized to a wider framework of action chains. Yet in chapter IX, we were concerned with the vital distinction between *direct* and *indirect* bringing-about.[23] We now ask: is there not some way that this distinction could be modelled in the framework of the other two chapters? An answer is near to hand. We can easily define "direct bringing-about" as follows: p at W_j is *directly brought about at W_i* if, and only if p at W_j is brought about at W_i and W_j is at the very next stage of the tree from W_i. The notion of the "very next stage (or set of points)" on a tree is perfectly clear and unequivocal, and may be defined as follows: W_j is in the set of points *at the next stage from W_i* if, and only if $W_i <$ W_j and there is no point W_k ($W_k \neq W_i \neq W_j$) such that $W_i < W_k$ $< W_j$. Another equivalent way to define *the next stage* is permitted by the device we outlined at the close of the section, Possible Outcome Trees and Inevitability, in which we ranked the set of points on a tree by a time-ranking, $t_0, t_1, \ldots t_k$.[24] The idea here is that *direct bringing-about* at W_j in relation to W_i is simply "one-step" bringing-about. Then we could say that a bringing-about of p is indirect if and only if it is not direct. By this means we can extend our theory of action chains of this chapter in the direction of partially, at least, expressing the notion of a "one-step" action that takes place at a specific time (or shorter interval of time). Thus we can also partly model the "pushiness" of action even though our theory is primarily directed to "spread-out" action-chains over longer sequences of possible outcomes.

Take the example of my firing a gun by pulling the trigger. This may be thought of as a "direct" or "one-step" action. Of course, what we consider to be a one-step interval over a tree is rather an arbitrary matter and is relativized to our interest in breaking a sequence down into a series of steps (or "links" if you like). If our interest is moral responsibility, the firing of the gun may appropriately be viewed as a direct sequence, i.e., other "bringings-about" such as the bullet's piercing a target are indirect in relation to my pulling the

23. See also Walton (1976b).
24. See also Åqvist (1974).

trigger compared to the firing of the gun which is relatively direct. The familiar idea is that some consequences are less remote than others in relation to a given action. But if our interest is ballistics, the firing of the gun may be relatively indirect in relation to the pulling of the trigger. As intervening steps we may have, for example, the falling of the hammer, the striking of the shell by the hammer, the ignition of the charge in the cartridge, etc. The actual firing, thought of perhaps as the explosion of the powder, is according to this interest, thought of as suitably indirect. Nevertheless, even though the isolation and demarcation of a set of stages in an action chain is a process that contains a certain arbitrariness and vagueness of application and is not defined exactly as "literally the next instant," the breaking down of actions into steps or stages may be exhibited in a sequential structure of the type we propose in a very natural way. And accordingly we may define a relative notion of proximity of stages according to which one stage may be thought of as relatively remote or near as compared to a third stage along the same chain. Obviously the "chain," the ordering of a sequence into a discrete set of "links" must be thought of as given. But given a chain, we can order the points on it by the appropriate relations defined in our theory. Thus to a certain extent at least, we can model the direct-indirect distinction in an interesting and instructive way within the theory.

Concluding Remarks on Action Theory

We started in the previous chapters with a distinction between "bringing-about" and "letting-happen" that probably initially seemed clear and forceful intuitively, but that has now been shown to be rather forbiddingly complex. The medical practitioner or medical ethicist, quite justifiably fearing entrapment in the coils of finely drawn scholastic or logical distinctions, might at this point prefer to abandon the idiom of bringing-about altogether. The argument might be expressed: surely we do not need to get involved in the philosophical complexities of the language of bringing-about and letting-happen. After all, the fundamental issue is that of weighing our values of, for instance, saving life or alleviating suffering, against the various possible outcomes of a situation. And surely we can do this without utilizing the words "bringing about" or "allowing to happen." Therefore all these philosophical complexities are redundant. Now I would like to express a certain degree of sympathy with this argument. Certainly those writers in medical ethics who have tried to put a heavy burden on this sort of distinction in their ethical arguments might now well begin to question whether the distinction is clear or straightforward enough to support their views in the way they thought. But I would doubt whether the ethical problems at issue can be stated in any language that does not after all turn out to be equivalent at least in large part to the linguistic framework outlined in this chapter. For example, one might argue that the ethical issues can be more perspicuously framed in the language of decision theory. Surely we are here simply trying to weigh up the various values to the patient, family, and others concerned, in relation to the various probable outcomes. But notice that standard forms of the language of decision theory and games theory are "decision trees" or "games trees,"[25] which are indeed closely equivalent in logical form to the framework proposed above. Thus I think it is harder to avoid the language of bringing-about than it may seem. The basic notion of bringing-about is such a fundamental, primitive category of all practical human thinking that it is virtually impossible to avoid recourse to it in some form in practical or ethical reasoning. So I agree that it would be desirable to avoid the language of action if some clearer, more exact, equally expressive language were available for us to utilize as a vehicle for conducting these medico-legal ethical deliberations. But insofar as such languages might be available, e.g., from decision theory, they are likely to share considerable structure with ours. Indeed, it would now be an interesting and useful exercise in developing the framework of this chapter further by showing much more exactly how it is related to existing formalisms in modal logic, algebra, and decision theory.

Perhaps it is needless to add that in our efforts to bring some discipline of logic to bear on the notoriously emotional and controversial questions of medical ethics and death, we are trying to achieve an interdisciplinary meeting of theory and practice that will leave significant gaps. At its present state of development, the topic is not a "safe" one. But it is often urged that the philosopher should

25. See R. D. Luce and H. Raiffa, *Games and Decisions: Introduction and Critical Survey* (New York: Wiley, 1957).

address himself to the much-discussed ethical problems of death, and yet do so without usurping the substantive roles of the health-care practitioner, the lawyer, and other colleagues. Thus the philosophical analyst's principal task is to enucleate the underlying conceptual structure and fundamental principles on which the life-or-death decisions are based. He must find (a) the abstract principles, analyze them in a way that is adequately clear and consistent by his standards, and yet (b) at the same time try to show or at least indicate how these abstract principles can fit into and apply to some real-life cases that the more practical disciplines are actually confronted with on a day-to-day basis. If he fails to meet (a), his efforts do not meet the basic requirements of philosophical analysis and may be systematically rejected on grounds of logic and internal coherence. But if he fails to meet (b), his efforts will be dismissed as simply irrelevant. And perhaps this is the crueler fate. By determinedly attempting to grapple with problems of death and dying from both ends, the best I can have hoped to accomplish here is to have set out a preliminary basis for further dialogue among the various disciplines concerned in order to encourage communication to develop along constructive, more objective lines.

Chapter XI

Is It Rational to Fear Death?

In previous chapters we investigated the conditions under which death might reasonably be thought to be an object of negative evaluation, and this investigation in turn raises the question of how and whether death might reasonably be thought to be fearful. Of course, the question of whether or not people do actually exhibit emotions of fear or anxiety in response to death-stimuli is an empirical-psychological question that can only be determined by the methods of empirical psychology or by psychiatric methods, and has indeed been the object of recent investigations. (See, for example, Lester, 1967 and 1970.) But the question of how one *should* react to the fact of death is a normative-philosophical question, to a certain extent independent of the psychological question.

Kinds of Thanatophobia

One interesting aspect of the dual view of death is the relation between it and a topic that has been studied in some detail, namely that of attitudes toward death, and in particular, fear of death. Some very brief comments may be in order. Kastenbaum and Aisenberg (1972, p. 45) distinguish three kinds of (self-oriented) death-related fears, *dying*, *afterlife*, and *extinction*. On our account of the secular hypothesis, the first is irrelevant (at least directly) to fear of death, the second is simply otiose (as the Stoics and Epicureans pointed out repeatedly), but the third becomes philosophically puzzling. Do we mean by "fear of extinction" fear of the loss of a valuable life? That is, is extinction an object of avoidance because its possible alternative, continued life, is an object of positive attraction? This kind of fear, or at least aversion, is easily explained and understood on the superlimiting view. Intuitively, however, over and above this kind of aversion, there seems to be an instinctive horror of the abyss, a fear of annihilation of the ego, a fear of "ceasing to be." Philosophers may well want to question whether this fear is rational, since it appears to stem from an unwarranted hypostatization of death (making nothing into something, so to speak). According to the limiting conception, we have no first-hand experience of death at all, and therefore it is highly misleading on this view to say that there is a nothing or void that we might actually experience. We can, of course, make the inference, each of us individually, that he or she will cease to exist as an actual person (with overwhelming probability), but apart from the value of the alternative, why should ceasing to exist be, in itself, a rational object of fear or aversion?[1] We will not attempt to answer this difficult question here. Much depends, for one thing, on the standards of rationality that are adopted. But the dual conception of death allows us to formulate this and related questions on thanatophobia and attitudes towards death in a clearer way than we could previously. In a skeptical spirit, we ask: What conceivable rational justification could be given for fearing "ceasing to be" on the superlimiting theory?

There are certain kinds of thanatophobia that are actually inconsistent with the dual conception of death. One kind of fear marked for special consideration by Kastenbaum and Aisenberg (1972, p. 47) is the possibility that a person will actually experience the moment of his own death. At least literally, this possibility is simply ruled out by the limiting aspect of the dual view. Other kinds of fear sometimes cited also come out to be irrational (in the sense of being logically inconsistent) with assumptions inherent in the dual view. For example, fear of death as some form of painful experience is

1. No doubt cessation of existence is an object of fear that may even, from a psychiatric viewpoint, be fairly well defined in a person's consciousness. But the question we pose here is how such a fear could be rationally justified. No justification would seem forthcoming on the superlimiting theory, according to which negative valuation of an outcome is to be sought exclusively in the possibility of attaching a positive value to an alternative. But the alternative to mere non-existence is not necessarily pleasant or worthwhile continued existence. We do not argue that no justification for negative valuation can be given, but we do feel that since no obvious candidate is available on the dual view, a certain skepticism is justified. As the Epicureans and Stoics repeatedly ask: why should we fear ceasing to be? It would seem to be of no concern to us, barring some argument to the contrary.

simply ruled out by the dual view. Death is mere projection or possibility, and consequently any assumption that death occurs within experience is simply inconsistent. Hence the ancient Stoic and Epicurean arguments: death is beyond sensation and therefore not a rational object of fear on the grounds of being painful. It is not an unpleasant experience, since, of course, it is not experienced at all.

Next we turn to some related arguments for and against the rationality of fear of death that require clarification and evaluation. To a certain extent, these arguments are similar to ones already examined, but they introduce some new considerations and different points of view. Some of these arguments are very ancient.

Thanatophobia and Nothing

One of the most interesting and forceful arguments for not fearing death is found in Plato. Socrates argues in a famous passage, the *Apology* (40d), that if the dead lack consciousness, as in a dreamless sleep, then they can hardly be said to be in pain or unhappy in any respect. Socrates even suggests, as a kind of corollary, that since duration could not be experienced in such a deep sleep, death could not be a troublesome period to pass through, as the whole of time would be equivalent to a single night as far as the dead are concerned.

> Death is one of two things. Either it is annihilation, and the dead have no consciousness of anything, or, as we are told, it is really a change—a migration of the soul from this place to another. Now if there is no consciousness but only a dreamless sleep, death must be a marvelous gain. I suppose that if anyone were told to pick out the night on which he slept so soundly as not even to dream, and then to compare it with all the other nights and days of his life, and then were told to say, after due consideration, how many better and happier days and nights than this he had spent in the course of his life—well, I think that the Great King himself, to say nothing of any private person, would find these days and nights easy to count in comparison with the rest. If death is like this, then, I call it gain, because the whole of time, if you look at it in this way, can be regarded as no more than one single night.

These arguments are also found in the Stoics. Marcus Aurelius taught that when being overtaken by death a man should reflect on the shortness of life and the chasm of time before and after, and that no evil can befall a man in death, if death is complete lack of consciousness.

The central thrust of this argument runs as follows: on the secular view of death, fear of it may be due to the fear of the irreversible extinction of consciousness. Yet such a fear is irrational—there is literally nothing to be afraid of. If consciousness is totally and permanently extinguished, the dead have no experience or awareness of anything, and it seems irrational to fear this. The state of being dead is not a painful, unpleasant, or fearful experience—it is simply not experienced. A possible rejoinder to the argument is that it is this very emptiness—the total extinction of awareness—that is feared. But how can we fear *nothing?* Well, we can and sometimes do fear being deprived of something we desire. Most of us would fear blindness—deprivation of sight. We might fear the loss of a loved one. Similarly, on a grander scale, we fear the loss of everything—death. As a total and permanent loss and deprivation of everything, death is fearful indeed, or so the counter-argument runs.[2]

To a certain extent, this argument represents a repetition of ones we have already dealt with. Death is not painful, on the dual view, or any like secular view, as we have seen, because death itself is not actually experienced. As for the factor of deprivation, we have seen that this can be accounted for as a legitimate object of negative valuation on the dual view where survival has a positive value for the individual. But third, the argument also seems to trade on the fearfulness of the sheer cessation of actual existence and annihilation of the ego that is a consequence of the strict secular conception of death. We have seen, however, that it is not obvious how it might be made out that this is a rational object of fear, even if from a psychiatric viewpoint it is easy to see how it could be fear-inducing. Moreover, an ancient rebuttal is ready at hand—why fear cessation of existence if you will not even exist at the time of what is allegedly fearful is to take place? Something of the flow of the arguments can be mapped out in a pattern of three traditional types of positions.

2. We might call this the argument from total deprivation.

Three Arguments

Argument 1: only the painful is fearful. By pain we include not only physical pain but also emotional pain such as the pain of bereavement. If this thesis obtains, then death should not be feared since the dead feel no pain (although the process of dying may be painful).
Argument 2: being deprived of something is fearful. According to this thesis the class of fearful things includes not only painful things, but also deprivations in themselves. If this thesis obtains, death might be feared since it consists of a form of deprivation of all existence.[3]
Rebuttal to Argument 2: being deprived of something you desire is only fearful if you are going to be present to experience the pain of deprivation. The prospect of being deprived of a loved one, is only fearful if you will be around actually to experience the loss. If death entails total lack of experience, there will be no awareness in death of the loss of life and what is valued in life, and thus there will be no actual experience of loss to be fearful of.
Support of Argument 2 against Rebuttal: a potential loss may be fearful even if you will not actually experience it. For example, being separated from a loved one seems a reasonable cause of some emotion in the prospect—perhaps even fear, or at any rate anxiety—even if one will not experience the separation when it occurs (or even if both parties will not experience it).

Before returning to the evaluation of Arguments 1 and 2 let us digress briefly to examine a third argument that, while worth our attention, is in my opinion not nearly so difficult as the issues represented by the above two and can therefore be dismissed relatively summarily.
Argument 3: a life span longer than the normal is not desirable for the rational person. Hence it is not rational to fear at least non-premature death. This argument is common enough, and it is argued on various grounds—a life span longer than the normal is said to be tedious, repetitious, aesthetically unpleasant, socially undesirable, and so on. Thus death is not to be feared but welcomed, in principle, in all cases. Three classical formulations of this argument are particularly interestingly stated. The first is due to Hartshorne (1958, p. 387).

3. Death is thought of here not merely as the deprivation of a worthwhile continued existence, but as a total deprivation of all existence altogether. Thus this argument may be independent of the counterlimit thesis.

No animal endowed with much power of memory ought to live forever, or could want to, I should maintain; for the longer it lives, the more that just balance between novelty and repetition, which is the basis of zest and satisfaction, must be upset in favor of repetition, hence of monotony and boredom. Old animals, and old people, in principle (exceptions are in degrees only) are bored animals and bored people. This is not essentially a glandular or circulatory phenomenon. It is psychological: One has felt and done most of the things that must be felt and done so many times before.

As Jefferson wrote to a friend: "I am tired of putting my clothes on every morning and taking them off every evening." Thus, he concluded, the Creator prepares us for death. Thus indeed. That many old people are spry and eager only proves that their chronological age gives but a rough index of psychological age. Thus all complaint against death itself seems misguided. Death is needed for the solution of an aesthetic problem, how memory is to be reconciled with zest.

A second interesting variation on the same theme can be found in Swift's *Gulliver's Travels* in Part III, ch. X, the voyage to Luggnagg. In this country, from time to time and purely at random a child is born with a distinctive mark on its forehead. Such an individual— called a *Struldbrugg*—has the property of being immortal. The *Struldbruggs* comprise only a very small minority of the population of Luggnagg. One would expect, Gulliver speculates, that the *Struldbruggs*, being exempt from the apprehension of death and having the opportunity to accumulate wealth and the wisdom of former ages, to be illustrious and superior beings. The picture Swift sketches is quite the opposite. The *Struldbruggs* are normal until thirty, after which age they become dejected, opinionated, peevish, covetous, morose, vain, talkative, unsociable, and envious, particularly of the dead. Eventually they lose their teeth, hair, appetite, memory, and ability to communicate. As they grow old they are ghastly to see and are universally despised and hated. It is pointed out to Gulliver that only in those countries not having *Struldbruggs* is death considered an evil to be delayed as long as possible. Once Gulliver recognizes that his previous favorable picture of eternal life included the impossible assumption of eternal youth, health, and vigor, he is reconciled to the irrationality of the desire to postpone death even if it approaches late.

A third argument of this type is found in Voltaire's *Micromégas*. An inhabitant of Saturn laments that the people on his planet live only to fifteen thousand years. "So, you see, we in a manner begin to die at the very moment we are born: our existence is no more than a point, our duration an instant, and our globe an atom. Scarce do we begin to learn a little, when death intervenes before we can profit by experience: for my own part, I am deterred from laying any schemes. I consider myself as a single drop in an immense ocean." The inhabitant of Sirius replies that inhabitants of his planet live seven hundred times longer than on Saturn. Moreover, he adds that he has been in some countries where people live a thousand times longer than Sirians, and still complained about the shortness of life. He concludes that when the moment of death arrives, there is not the least difference between having lived a whole eternity or a single day. The same argument is also found in Marcus Aurelius.

I do not wish to dwell overlong on Argument 3 here because I believe that it merits less serious attention than the issues raised by Arguments 1 and 2, so suffice it to marshal several brief points in rebuttal, five of which may be found in Lamont's admirable article (1965), required reading for serious inquirers in this area.

1. Nobody desires eternal senility. It is nevertheless quite reasonable to wish to live forever in good health and other favorable conditions.

2. Old animals may get bored, but people, or some of them, are different. There are endless opportunities for an educated man to enjoy continued novelty and zest.

3. It is simply false that repetition, *as such*, leads to boredom, e.g., consider the basic biological drives.

4. Memories do not always lead to boredom, but sometimes to a desire for repetition.

5. Constant repetition of the identical experience may lead to boredom, but a repeated *cycle of variety* does not have the same effect.

6. It may well be true that when the moment of death arrives we still wish to live longer, no matter how long we have lived [contra Swift], yet it does not follow that such a wish is unreasonable. We appear to have an unlimited capacity to enjoy pleasant experiences.

7. A life of Kn years and degree of pleasantness Kp is more desirable than a life of n years of pleasantness p, even though a reasonable person might be equally loath to die in either case [put in any number > 1 for K].

Perhaps these considerations suffice to rebut Argument 3. In any case, we conclude that under certain conditions it appears to remain reasonable to wish to extend life beyond the normal span if this were possible, and return to a consideration of some issues raised by Arguments 1 and 2.

Rationality

The anterior question arises—is it ever rational to fear anything? A related question—would a perfectly rational person (an idealization) ever fear anything? Suppose we characterize a rational person as one who always maximizes his expected utilities—then the second question appears to be equivalent to the empirical question—is fear ever a pragmatic or useful emotion (conducive to greater probable benefits)?

Provided that it is reasonable to fear losing something you desire, then from a games-theoretic point of view it is reasonable to fear death, if life has some value for you.[4] If death entails a total lack of experience or feelings then the value of any outcome for a person in that state should be exactly zero. Whereas if the total value of a given set of outcomes for a living person having expectations, desires, wishes, and other feelings is greater than zero, then it is reasonable for him to fear death.

But can the concept of rationality involved in the question of thanatophobia adequately be explicated on the standard games-theoretic models? It might seem not, but in this case, in what direction can we turn for an explication of this key term? I think we might expect great divergence of opinion on how to proceed here— my own suggestion is that games-theoretic models, while limited in their power to express a full range of concepts of rationality, are an obvious and fruitful beginning point for further exploration.

4. Here the counterlimit thesis comes into play.

Rational and Irrational Fears

We might distinguish between rational and irrational fears by example. Given various evidences of a tiger in a certain wood, it might be reasonable so fear attack by the tiger, but given that, say, I am in a wood in northern Manitoba where it is very unlikely that a tiger will appear, it would be irrational to fear attack by a tiger. In this case, the agent's fear is irrational because his estimate of the probability of a certain painful occurrence is incommensurate with the evidence. In other cases, his estimate of the painfulness of the consequences of a certain (probable) outcome may result in an irrational fear. A young child's fear of innoculation may be said to be irrational not because he is mistaken about the likelihood of his being inocculated tomorrow, but because he imagines it is a much more physically painful experience than it in fact is. Thus an irrational fear of an outcome, R, occurs when the agent either estimates that R is either more painful or more likely (or both) than the total evidence warrants. Since for any given person, death, at some time or other, is a virtual certainty, it is impossible to over-estimate its likelihood. Thus if fear of death is irrational, it must be through exaggeration of its painfulness. If being dead is, on the secular hypothesis, not painful at all, then any degree of fear of death is irrational.

Control of Fear

Can we control fear? It is the experience of many combat soldiers that nearly all normal persons are afraid in combat, but the difference between the good and bad soldier is that the former learns to do the job anyway, despite the fear. At any rate, it seems to be a reasonably plausible empirical thesis that fear cannot be entirely controlled, but at best contained. On the other hand, if we defined "influence" as probabilistic control,[5] it seems reasonable that fear can be influenced. In particular, we can train ourselves to react calmly to certain types

5. We might say that we control a state of affairs R, if we can guarantee that it will come about, whereas we can influence R's occurring if we can make it more likely that R will come about, or less likely, in the case of negative influence. See Rescher (1969).

of fear-inducing situations, so that when one of these situations occurs we will react less fearfully. Thus generally, it seems that we can influence, if not control fear, but it remains whether we can control it in a given particular case. In a particular case, our fear-reducing training, it might be said, does not allow us to control the amount of fear we experience in that situation; our training simply causes us to feel less fear in that situation. What this indicates is that control of fear may be a fairly long-term process. On the other hand, one might conceivably use various short-term methods in a particular short-term situation, a crude example of which would be counting to ten or some such attention-diverting device. A borderline case is the athlete whose hand shakes where he requires a steady hand in a competition such as markmanship. In getting his hand to stop shaking, does he control his fear of losing or simply contain it? In the spirit of the soldiers case, we might say that he has not controlled or checked his fear of losing, but simply learned to cope with it and get along in spite of it. This raises the issue of whether fear can be defined by a set of empirical measurements such as pulse rate, galvanic skin response etc., or whether these properties are simply manifestations of an emotion or mental state.[6]

It is sometimes said that we fear the unknown.[7] But is not our fear due to the fact that a situation of uncertainty may result in painful experiences? It is not the unknown as such that is feared, but the likelihood that an unfamiliar situation might result in unforseen painful experiences. Normally we can be fairly confident in familiar situations that nothing very painful is likely to happen (only otherwise is fear justified) and so normally we can relax our fears.[8] But in a situation of uncertainty, we cannot be so confident that painful experiences will not appear, and our fear is therefore increased. In a situation of positive likelihood of harm, our fear will be even greater than in the unknown case.[9] Of course, in the unknown case, a person (say a neurotic), might exaggerate the likely degree of painfulness of the consequences, but this would be a case of irrational fear.

6. See Kastenbaum and Aisenberg (1972), Chasin (1971), and Crown, O'Donovan, and Thompson (1967).
7. See Durlak (1973) and Feifel and Branscomb (1973) for some related questions.
8. See Glaser and Strauss (1966).
9. See Gordon (1970) and Green and Irish (1971).

Concluding Remarks

We conclude that Argument 3 may be rejected, whereas Arguments 1 and 2 pose an opposition that can only be definitively settled or clarified by further investigation into the concepts *death*, *fear*, and *rational*. The third concept, in particular, poses a source of considerable ambiguity and slippage.[10] Anatol Rapoport once pointed out that, contrary to a common view, there is no single concept of rationality but very many such concepts, and in particular many such games-theoretic concepts. Despite such qualifications, we wish to suggest that Argument 1 maintains a good deal of preanalytic promise—it remains intuitively implausible that one might rationally fear a completely unexperienceable lack. Though nothing conclusive we have put forward rules out the counter-thesis, Argument 2— namely that a total cessation of existence might rationally be feared even if it could not be experienced during the time of actual deprivation[11]—we should add that the degree of fear most of us would think reasonable under Argument 2 would perhaps not be nearly so great as fear of death commonly seems to be. To be sure, on the counter-limit thesis, it is reasonable to evaluate death negatively where a continuation of life is of positive value, but it is questionable whether death should always be an object of very high negative value on this criterion. Socrates, for example, is known to have been influenced by his advancing age and declining abilities in making his decision to die voluntarily. Furthermore, on the secular hypothesis, it is blatant inconsistency to fear death on the ground that it will be any kind of painful experience or that any harm can come to an individual in death, for on that hypothesis, the actual individual simply ceases to exist and can undergo no experiences whatever.

Thus one way to pass between the *Scylla* and *Charybdis* of Arguments 1 and 2 is that a certain modicum of apprehension or anxiety about death is reasonable, consonant with the undesirability, indeed the tragedy, of being deprived of the continuation of a worthwhile, pleasant life. What is feared under such an interpretation, we might say, is not death in itself, but the discontinuation of a valuable life. To be so preoccupied to the point where the other phases of life are interfered with, to fear death as a child fears the dark, mistakenly to

10. On irrationality of fear, see Kastenbaum and Aisenberg (1972, pp. 55–65).
11. Except, of course, the Stoic rebuttal that it is absurd to fear something that is alleged to occur at a time when you yourself do not even exist.

associate death with suffering and pain, to be in rage or existential
angst about death, are attitudes that, on the secular conception, lack
a rational basis for the reasonable, honest, and reflective person. It
may be fitting to close with an inspirational quotation from Bertrand
Russell's *New Hopes for a Changing World*:

> Some old people are oppressed by the fear of death. In the
> young there is a justification for this feeling. Young men who
> have reason to fear that they will be killed in battle may justifi-
> ably feel bitter in the thought that they have been cheated of the
> best things that life has to offer. But in an old man who has
> known human joys and sorrows, and has achieved whatever
> work it was in him to do, the fear of death is somewhat abject
> and ignoble. The best way to overcome it—so at least it seems to
> me—is to make your interests gradually wider and more
> impersonal, until bit by bit the walls of the ego recede, and your
> life becomes increasingly merged in the universal life. An
> individual human existence should be like a river—small at
> first, narrowly contained within its banks, and rushing passion-
> ately past boulders and over waterfalls. Gradually the river
> grows wider, the banks recede, the waters flow more quietly, and
> in the end, without any visible break, they become merged in the
> sea, and painlessly lose their individual being. The man who, in
> old age, can see his life in this way, will not suffer from the fear
> of death, since the things he cares for will continue. And if, with
> the decay of vitality, weariness increases, the thought of rest will
> be not unwelcome.

Philosophers have traditionally given us advice, much of it valuable,
on how to cope with the fear of death. Russell's has always struck me
as being particularly sensible. My own bit of advice, for what it is
worth, would be to suggest trying to understand, clearly and
logically, what exactly is fearful about death, without however
letting this philosophical exercise become a morbid preoccupation.

Bibliography

Other useful bibliographies are to be found in Kutscher and Kutscher (1969), Brand (1970), Gruman (1973), Harp (1974), Clouser and Zucker (1974), Van Till (1975 and 1976), and Walters (1975).

ALEXANDER, L.
1949   Medical Science Under Dictatorship. *New England Journal of Medicine*, 241: 39–47.

ALEXANDRE, G. P. J.
1966   Transplantation: Practical Possibilities (discussion). In *Ciba Foundation Symposium: Ethics in Medical Progress*. Ed. G. E. W. Wolstenholme. Boston: Little, Brown & Co., p. 69.

AMENT, W. R.
1972   Constitutional Law—Compulsory Medical Treatment for an Adult— The Right of an Adult to Refuse Lifesaving Medical Treatment Based Upon the Free Exercise Clause of the First Amendment. *Duquesne Law Review*, 11: 242–53.

ANSELM, SAINT, OF CANTERBURY
1969   *Memorials of St. Anselm*. Ed. F. S. Schmitt and R. W. Southern. London: Oxford University Press.

ÅQVIST, LENNART
1973   Modal Logic with Subjunctive Conditionals and Dispositional Predicates. *Journal of Philosophical Logic*, 2: 1–76.
1973a *Kausalitet och Culpaansvar inom en Logiskt Rekonstruerad Skadeståndsrätt.* Uppsala University. Philosophical Studies, Uppsala, Sweden.
1974   A New Approach to the Logical Theory of Actions and Causality. In *Logical Theory and Semantics*, ed. Sören Stenlund. Dordrecht: Reidel, pp. 73–91.

ARIÈS, PHILIPPE
1974   Death Inside Out. *Hastings Center Studies*, 2: 3–18 (trans. by B. Murchland).
1975   Les Grandes Etapes et le Sens de l'Evolution de nos Attitudes devant la Mort. *Archives de Sciences Sociales des Religions*, 39: 7–16.

AURELIUS, MARCUS
1963   *The Meditations*. Trans. G. M. A. Grube. Indianapolis: Bobbs-Merrill.

AYD, F., JR.
1970   Voluntary Euthanasia: the Right to be Killed. *Medical Counterpoint*, June,
       p. 12.

BAIER, ANNETTE
1971   The Search for Basic Actions. *American Philosophical Quarterly*, 8: 161–70.

BEAUCHAMP, TOM L.
1975   A Defense of the Distinction Between Active and Passive Euthanasia.
       Unpublished paper, Georgetown University, Department of
       Philosophy.

BEECHER, HENRY K.
1968   A Definition of Irreversible Coma. Report of the Ad Hoc Committee
       of the Harvard Medical School to Examine the Definition of Brain
       Death. *Journal of the American Medical Association*, 205: 337–40.
1968a Ethical Problems Created by the Hopelessly Unconscious Patient.
       New England Journal of Medicine, 278: 1415–30.
1970   Definitions of "Life" and "Death" for Medical Science and Practice.
       Annals of the New York Academy of Sciences, 169, Article 2: 471–74.

BEECHER, HENRY K., and DORR, HENRY ISAIAH
1971   The New Definition of Death: Some Opposing Views, *Internationale
       Zeitschrift fur Klinische Pharmakologie, Therapie und Toxikologie*, 5: 120–24.

BEHNKE, JOHN A., and BOK, SISSELA
1975   *The Dilemmas of Euthanasia*. Garden City, N.Y.: Anchor Press/
       Doubleday.

BENNETT, JONATHAN
1966   Whatever the Consequences. *Analysis*, 26: 83–102. Reprinted in
       Rachels (1971), and Gorovitz et al. (1976).

BERMAN, A. L., and HAYS, J. E.
1973   Relation between Death Anxiety, Belief in Afterlife, and Locus of
       Control. *Journal of Consulting and Clincal Psychology*, 41: 318.

BERNSTEIN, ARTHUR
1972   Consent to Operate, to Live, or to Die. *Hospitals*, 46: 124–28.

BOK, SISSELA
1976   Personal Directions for Care at the End of Life. *New England Journal
       of Medicine*, 295: 367–69.

BRAND, MYLES
1970   *The Nature of Human Action*. Glenview: Illinois, Scott, Foresman.
1971   The Language of Not Doing. *American Philosophical Quarterly*, 8: 45–53.

BRAND, MYLES, and WALTON, DOUGLAS
1976   *Action Theory*. Dordrecht: Reidel.

BRAUNSTEIN, P., KOREIN, J., et al.
1973   A Simple Bedside Evaluation for Cerebral Blood Flow in the Study of
        Cerebral Death: A Prospective Study on 34 Deeply Comatose
        Patients. *American Journal of Roentgenology*, 118: 757–67.

BRODY, BARUCH
1975   *Abortion and the Sanctity of Human Life: A Philosophical View.* Cambridge,
        Mass.: MIT Press.

BUCHELER, E., and KAUFER, C.
1972   Karotis and Vertebralisangiographie Beim Hirntod. *Acta Radiologica*,
        13: 301–10.

CANNON, WILLIAM F.
1970   The Right to Die. *Houston Law Review*, 7: 654–70.

CANTOR, NORMAN L.
1973   Patient's Decision to Decline Life-Saving Medical Treatment: Bodily
        Integrity Versus the Preservation of Life. *Rutgers Law Review*, 26:
        228–64.

CAPRON, ALEXANDER, M., and KASS, LEON R.
1972   A Statutory Definition of the Standards for Determining Human
        Death. *University of Pennsylvania Law Review*, 121: 87–118.

CAPRON, ALEXANDER M.
1973   The Purpose of Death: A Reply to Professor Dworkin. *Indiana Law
        Journal*, 48: 640–46.

CARNAP, RUDOLF
1950   *Logical Foundations of Probability.* Chicago: University of Chicago Press
        (2nd ed. 1962).

CARTWRIGHT, ANN, et al.
1973   *Life Before Death.* Boston: Routledge and Kegan Paul.

CASSELL, ERIC, KASS, LEON R., et al.
1972   Refinements in Criteria for the Determination of Death: An Appraisal.
        A Report by the Task Force on Death and Dying of the Institute of
        the Society, Ethics, and the Life Sciences. *Journal of the American
        Medical Association*, 221: 48–53.

CASSELL, ERIC J.
1974   Dying in a Technological Society. *Hastings Center Studies*, 2: 31–36.
1975   Preliminary Explorations of Thinking in Medicine. *Ethics in Science and
        Medicine*, 2: 1–12.

CASSEM, NED H.
1975   Controversies Surrounding the Hopelessly Ill Patient. *The Linacre
        Quarterly*, 42: 89–98.

CHASIN, B.
1971   Neglected Variables in the Study of Death Attitudes. *Sociological
        Quarterly*, 12: 107–13.

CHISHOLM, RODERICK
1964   The Descriptive Element in the Concept of Action. *Journal of Philosophy*. LXI: 613–25.
1969   Some Puzzles About Agency. In *The Logical Way of Doing Things*, ed. Karel Lambert. New Haven: Yale University Press, pp. 199–217.

CHURCH INFORMATION OFFICE
1975   On Dying Well—An Anglican Contribution to the Debate on Euthanasia, Working Party Report Under the Auspices of the Church of England's Board for Social Responsibility. London.

CHORON, JACQUES
1963   *Death and Western Thought*. London: Collier-Macmillan.

CLARKE, JOHN
1971   John Hick's Resurrection. *Sophia*, 10: 18–22.

CLOUSER, K. DANNER, and ZUCKER, ARTHUR
1974   *Annotated Bibliography of Recent Writings on Abortion and Euthanasia*. Philadelphia: The Society for Health and Human Values.

CLOW, ARCHIE
1971   *Morals and Medicine*. New York: New York University Press.

CMAJ
1973   Manitoba Law Commission Proposes to Define Death Under Any Circumstances. *Canadian Medical Association Journal*, Editorial Report, 108: 381.

COFFEY, PATRICK
1976   When is Killing the Unborn a Homicidal Action? *The Linacre Quarterly*, 43: 85–93.

CONFERENCE OF MEDICAL ROYAL COLLEGES AND THEIR FACULTIES IN THE UNITED KINGDOM
1976   Diagnosis of Brain Death (Statement Issued by the Honorary Secretary of the Conference 11 October 1976). *British Medical Journal*, 2: 1187–88.

COOKE, ROBERT E.
1972   Whose Suffering? *Journal of Pediatrics*, 80: 906–7.

CROSBIE, S.
1969   Abortion and Euthanasia. *Rocky Mountain Medical Journal*, 66: 41–46.

CROWN, B., O'DONOVAN, D., and THOMPSON, T. G.
1967   Attitudes toward Attitudes toward Death. *Psychological Reports*, 20: 1181–82.

CULLITON, B. J.
1975   The Haemmerli Affair: Is Passive Euthanasia Murder? *Science*, 190: 1271–75.

CULLMANN, OSCAR
1958   *Immortality of the Soul or Resurrection of the Dead?* London: The Epworth Press.

CURRAN, CHARLES A.
1975   Death and Dying. *Journal of Religion and Health,* 14: 254–64.

CUTLER, DONALD A.
1968   *Updating Life and Death.* Boston: Beacon Press.

DANTO, ARTHUR
1965   Basic Actions. *American Philosophical Quarterly,* 2: 141–48.

DAVIDSON, DONALD
1966   The Logical Form of Action Sentences. In *The Logic of Decision and Action,* ed. Nicholas Rescher. Pittsburgh: University of Pittsburgh Press, pp. 81–85.
1971   Agency. In *Agent, Action and Reason,* ed. Robert Binkley, et al., Toronto: University of Toronto Press, pp. 3–25.

DAY, STACEY B.
1972   *Death and Attitudes Towards Death.* Bell Museum of Pathology, University of Minnesota Medical School.

DEGNER, LESLEY F.
1976   *The Life-Prolonging Dilemma: Its Impact on Patients, Families, and Health Practitioners.* Study Description, School of Nursing, University of Manitoba.

DEGNER, LESLEY F., and GLASS, HELEN P.
       Calculations of Risk Versus Benefit: Indicators in Health Care Decision-Making. Xeroxed paper, School of Nursing, University of Manitoba.

DINELLO, DANIEL
1971   On Killing and Letting Die. *Analysis,* 31: 84–86.

DIXON, JOHN
1975   "If a man dies, shall he live again?" : *The Christian Answer.* Photocopy, School of Administrative Studies, Canberra College of Advanced Education.

DOWNING, A. B.
1970   *Euthanasia and the Right to Die.* New York: Humanities Press.

DUCASSE, C. J.
1948   Is Life After Death Possible? The Agnes E. and Constantine E. Foerster Lecture, 1947. Copyright C. J. Ducasse, 1948. Reprinted in *Philosophy and Contemporary Issues.* Ed. John R. Burr and Milton Goldinger, New York: Macmillan, 1972.
1951   *Nature, Mind and Death.* LaSalle, Illinois: Open Court Publishing Co.
1961   *A Critical Examination of the Belief in a Life After Death.* Springfield, Ill.: Charles C. Thomas.

DUFF, R. A.
1973   Intentionally Killing the Innocent. *Analysis*, 34: 16–19.

DUFF, RAYMOND, and CAMPBELL, A. G. M.
1973   Moral and Ethical Dilemmas in the Special-Care Nursery. *New England Journal of Medicine*, 289: 890–94.

DURLAK, JOSEPH A.
1972   Measurement of the Fear of Death: An Examination of Some Existing Scales. *Journal of Clinical Psychology*, 28: 545–47.
1973   Relationship between Various Measures of Death Concern and Fear of Death. *Journal of Consulting and Clinical Psychology*, 41: 162.

DWORKIN, ROGER B.
1973   Death in Context. *Indiana Law Journal*, 48: 623–39.

EDITORIAL NOTE
1974   Informed Consent and the Dying Patient. *Yale Law Journal*, 83: 1632–64.

EDWARDS, PAUL
1967   My Death. Entry in Paul Edwards (ed.), *The Encyclopedia of Philosophy*, vol. 5. New York: Macmillan, pp. 416–19.
1976   Heidegger and Death: A Deflationary Critique. *The Monist*, 59: 161–86.
1977   *Death and Existentialism*. New York: The Free Press.

ENGLEHARDT, H. T., JR.
1973   Euthanasia and Children: The Injury of Continued Existence. *Journal of Pediatrics*, 83: 170–71.

EPICURUS
1964   *Letters, Principal Doctrines, and Vatican Sayings*. New York: Bobbs-Merrill.

EUTHANASIA EDUCATIONAL COUNCIL
1975   *A Living Will*. Euthanasia Educational Council, 250 West 57th Street, New York, N.Y. 10019.

FEIFEL, H., and BRANSCOMB, A. B.
1973   Who's Afraid of Death? *Journal of Abnormal Psychology*. 81: 282–88.

FEINBERG, JOEL
1965   Action and Responsibility. In *Philosophy in America*, ed. Max Black. London: Allen and Unwin, pp. 134–60.
1970   *Doing and Deserving*. Princeton, N.J.: Princeton University Press.
1976   *The Right to Life in Law and Morals*. Xeroxed bibliography. New York University School of Law.
1977   Harm and Self Interest. In J. Raz and P. Hacker (eds.), *Festschrift for H.L.A. Hart*. Oxford: Oxford University Press.

FITCH, FREDERIC B.
1963   A Logical Analysis of Some Value Concepts. *Journal of Symbolic Logic*, 28: 135–42.

FITZGERALD, P. J.
1967   Acting and Refraining. *Analysis*, 27: 133–39.

FLEMING, THOMAS B., et al.
1974   *Communication and Thanatology*. New York: Health Sciences Publishing Corporation.

FLETCHER, GEORGE
1967   Prolonging Life. *Washington Law Review*, 42: 999–1016.
1968   Legal Aspects of the Decision Not to Prolong Life. *Journal of the American Medical Association*, 203: 65–68.

FLETCHER, JOSEPH
1960   *Morals and Medicine*. Boston: Beacon Press.
1970   Voluntary Euthanasia: The New Shape of Death. *Medical Counterpoint*, June, p. 13.
1973   Medicine and the Nature of Man. *Science, Medicine and Man*, 1: 93–102.
1973a Ethics and Euthanasia. In *To Live and to Die*, ed. Robert H. Williams, New York: Springer, pp. 113–22.
1974   The "Right" to Live and the "Right" to Die: A Protestant View of Euthanasia. *The Humanist*, 34: 12–15.
1974a New Definitions of Death. *Prism*, January, pp. 13, 36.
1975   Abortion, Euthanasia, and Care of Defective Newborns. *New England Journal of Medicine*, 292: 75–78.

FLEW, ANTONY
1953   *A New Approach to Psychical Research*. London: Watts & Co.
1955   Theology and Falsification. In *New Essays in Philosophical Theology*, ed. Antony Flew, London: SCM Press, pp. 96–99.
1964   *Body, Mind, and Death*. New York: Macmillan.
1970   The Principle of Euthanasia. In Downing (1970), pp. 30–48.

FOOT, PHILIPPA
1967   The Problem of Abortion and the Doctrine of the Double Effect. *Oxford Review*, 5:5–15. Reprinted in Samuel Gorovitz et al. (eds.), *Moral Problems in Medicine*. Englewood Cliffs, N.J.: Prentice-Hall.

FREEMAN, JOHN
1972   Is there a Right to Die—Quickly? *Journal of Pediatrics*, 80: 905.

FRIEDMAN, H. R.
1976   Intimidations of Immortality. *The Monist*, 59: 234–48.

FURLOW, THOMAS W., JR.
1974   Tyranny of Technology: A Physician Looks at Euthanasia. *The Humanist*, 34: 6–8.

FULTON, ROBERT
1965   *Death and Identity*. New York, Wiley & Sons, Inc.

GEDDES, L.
1972   On the Intrinsic Wrongness of Killing Innocent People. *Analysis*, 33: 93–97.

GENOVA, A. C.
1973 Death as a Terminus Ad Quem. *Philosophy and Phenomenological Research*, XXXIV: 270–77.

GLASER, BARNEY G., and STRAUSS, ANSELM L.
1966 *Awareness of Dying*. Chicago: Aldine Publishing Co.

GOLDMAN, ALVIN
1970 *A Theory of Human Action*. Englewood Cliffs, N.J.: Prentice-Hall.

GOODRICH, T.
1969 The Morality of Killing. *Philosophy*, 44: 127–39.

GORDON, DAVID COLE
1970 *Overcoming the Fear of Death*. Baltimore, Maryland: Penguin Books.

GOROVITZ, SAMUEL
1975 Relating to Dying Patients. *American Review of Respiratory Disease*, 112: 159–63.

GOROVITZ, SAMUEL, et al.
1976 *Moral Problems in Medicine*. Englewood Cliffs, N.J.: Prentice-Hall.

GREEN, BETTY R., and IRISH, DONALD P.
1971 *Death Education: Preparation for Living*. Cambridge, Mass.: Schenkam Publishing Co.

GREEN, J. R.
1974 Brain Death, i.e., Irreversible Coma. *Arizona Medicine*, 31: 101.

GRISEZ, GERMAIN
1970 *Abortion: The Myths, the Realities, and the Arguments*. New York and Cleveland: Corpus Books.

GRUMAN, GERALD J.
1973 An Historical Introduction to Ideas About Voluntary Euthanasia: with a Bibliographic Survey and Guide for Interdisciplinary Studies. *Omega*, 4: 87–138.

HABGOOD, J. S.
1974 Euthanasia: A Christian View. *Royal Society of Health Journal*, 94: 118–22.

HALL, RONALD
1966 Analytic-Synthetic—A Bibliography. *Philosophical Quarterly*, 16: 178–81.

HALLEY, M., and HARVEY W.
1968 Medical vs. Legal Definitions of Death. *Journal of The American Medical Association*, 204: 103–5.

HARE, R. M.
1975 Euthanasia: A Christian View. *Philosophic Exchange*, 2: 43–53.

HARP, JAMES R.
1974 Criteria for the Determination of Death. *Anesthesiology*, 40: 391–97.

HART, H. L. A. and HONORÉ, A. M.
1969   *Causation in the Law*. Oxford: Oxford University Press.

HARTSHORNE, CHARLES
1958   Outlines of a Philosophy of Nature, Part II. *The Personalist*, 39: 380–91.

HEGLAND, KENNEY
1965   Unauthorized Rendition of Lifesaving Medical Treatment. *California Law Review*, 53: 860–77.

HEMPEL, CARL G.
1965   Empiricist Criteria of Cognitive Significance: Problems and Changes. *Aspects of Scientific Explanation*, Carl G. Hempel. New York: The Free Press.
1966   *Philosophy of Natural Science*. Englewood Clifs, N.J.: Prentice-Hall.

HENRY, DESMOND P.
1967   *The Logic of St. Anselm*. Oxford: Oxford University Press.

HICK, JOHN
1957   *Faith and Knowledge*. Ithaca, N.Y.: Cornell University Press. Also issued in Fontana Books, 1974.
1968   *Christianity at the Centre*. London: Macmillan.
1972   Mr. Clarke's Resurrection Also. *Sophia*, XI: 1–3.

HIGH, DALLAS M.
1972   Death: Its Conceptual Elusiveness. *Soundings*, 55: 438–58.

HILLMAN, H.
1972   Dying and Death (Editorial). *Resuscitation*, 1: 85–90.

HILPINEN, RISTO
1974   On the Semantics of Personal Directives. In *Semantics and Communication*, ed. Carl H. Heidrich, North-Holland: Amsterdam, 1974, pp. 162–79

HINTON, JOHN
1967   *Dying*. Harmondsworth, England: Penguin Books.

HOFLING, C. K.
1966   Terminal Decisions. *Medical Opinion and Review*, (October) 2: 40–49.

HOSSMAN, K. A., LECHTAPE-GRÜTER, H., and HOSSMAN, V.
1973   The Role of Cerebral Blood Flow for the Recovery of the Brain after Prolonged Ischemia. *Zeitschrift für Neurologie*, 204: 281–99.

HUGHES, G. E., and CRESSWELL, M. J.
1968   *An Introduction to Modal Logic*. London: Methuen.

INGVAR, D. H. et al.
1974   Report of the Committee on Cessation of Cerebral Function. *Electroencephalography and Clinical Neurophysiology*, 37: 530–31.

JACQUY, J., LACOGE, M., and MOUAWAD, E.
1974   Les Critères de la Mort Cérébrale. *Bruxelles-Médical*, 54: 385–86.

JAEGER, WERNER
1947   *The Theology of the Early Greek Philosophers*. Oxford: Oxford University
        Press.

JAMA
1968   What and When is Death? *Journal of the American Medical Association*,
        editorial, 204: 219–20.
1971   Euthanasia. *Journal of the American Medical Association*, editorial, 218:
        249.

JOHNSTONE, HENRY W., JR.
1975   Toward a Phenomenology of Death. *Philosophy and Phenomenological
        Research*, 35: 396–97.
1976   Sleep and Death. *The Monist*, 59: 218–33.

JONSEN, A. R.
1976   Ethicists' Heyday. *American Review of Respiratory Diseases*, 113: 5–6.

JØRGENSEN, PAUL B., JØRGENSEN, ERIKO, and ROSENKLINT, ARNE
1973   Brain Death Pathogenesis and Diagnosis. *Acta Neurologica Scandinavica*,
        49: 355–67.

JOSEPHS, DEBORAH
1971   The Right to Die with Dignity. *New York Times*, September 25.

JUUL-JENSEN, PALLE
1970   *Criteria of Brain Death: Selection of Donors for Transplantation* (trans. A.
        Rousing). Copenhagen: Munksgaard.

KAMISAR, YALE
1970   Euthanasia Legislation: Some Non-religious Objections. In Downing
        (1970), pp. 85–133.

KANGER, STIG
1972   Law and Logic. *Theoria*, 38: 105–32.

KANT, IMMANUEL
1963   Duties towards the Body in Regard to Life. In *Lectures on Ethics* (trans.
        L. Infield). New York: Harper & Row.

KASS, LEON R.
1971   Death as an Event: A Commentary on Robert Morison. *Science*, 1973:
        698–702.
1974   Averting One's Eyes, or Facing the Music?—On Dignity in Death.
        Hastings Center Studies, 2: 67–80.

KASTOVSKY, DIETER
1973   Causatives. *Foundations of Language*. 10: 255–315.

KASTENBAUM, ROBERT, and AISENBERG, RUTH
1972   *The Psychology of Death*. New York: Springer Verlag.

KELLY, G.
1950   The Duty of Using Artificial Means of Preserving Life. *Theological Studies*, 11: 203.
1958   *Medico-Moral Problems.* St. Louis: Catholic Hospital Association.

KENNEDY, IAN M.
1971   The Kansas Statute on Death: An Appraisal. *New England Journal of Medicine*, 285: 946–50.

KIM, JAEGWON
1974   Noncausal Connections. *Noûs*, 8: 41–52.

KLEINIG, JOHN
1976   Good Samaritanism. *Philosophy and Public Affairs*, 5: 382–407.

KLUGE, EIKE-HENNER W.
1975   *The Practice of Death.* New Haven and London: Yale University Press.

KOHL, MARVIN
1973   Understanding the Case for Beneficent Euthanasia, *Science, Medicine and Man.* 1: 111–21.
1974   *The Morality of Killing.* London: Peter Owen Ltd.
1974a   Beneficent Euthanasia. *The Humanist*, 34: 9–11.
1975   *Beneficent Euthanasia.* Buffalo, N.Y.: Prometheus.

KOVACS, GEORGE
1973   Man and Death: An Existential-Phenomenological Approach. *Proceedings of the American Catholic Philosophical Association*, 47: 183–90.

KRIEGER, SETH R., and EPTING, FRANZ R.
1974   Personal Constructs, Threats and Attitudes Towards Death. *Omega*, 5: 299–315.

KRIPKE, SAUL
1963   Semantical Analysis of Modal Logic I. *Zeitschrift für Mathematische Logik und Grundlagen der Mathematik*, 9: 69–96.

KRÖSL, W., and SCHERZER, E.
1973   *Die Bestimmung des Todeszeitpunktes.* Vienna: Wilhelm Maudrig Verlag.

KÜBLER-ROSS, ELISABETH
1969   *On Death and Dying.* New York: Macmillan.

KUTSCHER, AUSTIN H. JR., and KUTSCHER, AUSTIN H.
1969   *A Bibliography of Books on Death, Bereavement, Loss and Grief: 1935–1968.* New York: Health Sciences Publishing Corporation.

LABBY, D. H.
1968   *Life or Death: Ethics and Options.* Seattle: University of Washington Press.

LAMONT, CORLISS
1952   *The Illusion of Immortality.* London: Watts & Co.
1965   Mistaken Attitudes towards Death. *Journal of Philosophy,* LXII: 29–36.
1968   The Crisis Called Death. In Paul Kurtz (ed.), *Moral Problems in Contemporary Society.* Englewood Cliffs, N.J.: Prentice-Hall.

LANDSBERG, P. L.
1963   *The Experience of Death and the Moral Problem of Suicide.* London: Rockliff.

LANCET
1974   Brain Damage and Brain Death. *Lancet,* editorial, 1: 341–42.

LAWS, HAROLD E., et al.
1971   Views on Euthanasia. *Journal of Medical Education,* 46: 540–52.

LESTER, D.
1967   Experimental and Correlational Studies of the Fear of Death. *Psychological Bulletin,* 67: 27–36.
1970   The Need to Achieve and the Fear of Death. *Psychological Reports,* 27: 516.

LEWIS, DAVID
1968   Counterpart Theory and Quantified Modal Logic, *Journal of Philosophy,* 5: 113–26.
1971   Counterparts of Persons and their Bodies, *Journal of Philosophy,* 68: 203–11.
1973   *Counterfactuals.* Oxford: Blackwell.

LEWIS, H. P.
1968   Machine Medicine and its Relation to the Fatally Ill. *Journal of the American Medical Association,* 206: 387–88.

LEWIS, HYWEL D.
1973   *The Self and Immortality.* London and Basingstoke: Macmillan.

LIFTON, ROBERT JAY, and OLSON, ERIC
1974   *Living and Dying.* New York: Praeger Publishers, Inc.

MACHAN, TIBOR R.
1974   Recent Books on Euthanasia. *The Humanist,* 34: 40–41.

MACKIE, J. K.
1965   Causes and Conditions. *American Philosophical Quarterly,* 2: 245–64.

MAGUIRE, DANIEL C.
1974   *Death by Choice.* Garden City, N.Y.: Doubleday.
1974   A Catholic View of Mercy Killing. *The Humanist,* 34: 16–18.

MANNES, MARYA
1974   *Last Rights, A Case for the Good Death.* New York: William Morrow & Co.

MARGOLIS, JOSEPH
1975   *Negativities: The Limits of Life.* Columbus, Ohio: Charles E. Merrill.

MAY, WILLIAM
1972 The Sacral Power of Death in Contemporary Experience. *Social Research*, 39: 463–88.
1973 Attitudes Toward the Newly Dead. *Hastings Center Studies*, 1: 3–26.

MCCAWLEY, JAMES
1970 English as a VSO Language. *Language*, 46: 286–99.

MCCORMICK, RICHARD A.
1974 To Save or Let Die: The Dilemma of Modern Medicine. *Journal of the American Medical Association*, 229: 172–76.
1975 Life-Saving and Life-Taking: A Comment. *The Linacre Quarterly*, 42: 110–15.

MCINTYRE, R.
1970 Voluntary Euthanasia: The Ultimate Perversion. *Medical Counterpart*, June, p. 26.

MCKEGNEY, F., and LANGE, P.
1971 The Decision to No Longer Live on Chronic Hemodyalisis. *American Journal of Psychiatry*, 128: 267–74.

MEAD, MARGARET
1968 The Right to Die. *Nursing Outlook*, 16: 20–21.

MERRILL, J. P.
1971 A Declaration of the International Society of Transplantation. *Transplantation*, 12: 77–79.

MICHAEL, JEROME, and WECHSLER, HERBERT
1937 A Rationale of the Law of Homicide. *Columbia Law Review*, 37: 724–25.

MILLER, HENRY and BLOOM, ANTHONY
1971 Keeping People Alive. In Clow (1971), pp. 9–28.

MILLS, DON HARPER
1971 The Kansas Statute: Bold and Innovative. *New England Journal of Medicine*, 285: 968–69.

MOHANDAS, A., and CHOU, SHELLEY N.
1971 Brain Death: A Clinical and Pathological Study. *Journal of Neurosurgery*, 35: 211–18.

MONTAGUE, RICHARD
1974 *Formal Philosophy*. Ed. R. H. Thomason. New Haven: Yale University Press.

MORGAN, LUCY
1971 On Drinking the Hemlock. *Hastings Center Report*, 1: 4–5.

MORISON, ROBERT S.
1971 Death: Process or Event? *Science*, 173: 694–98.
1973 Dying. *Scientific American*. September, pp. 55–62.

MOTHERSILL, MARY
1971   Death. In James Rachels (ed.), *Moral Problems*, New York: Harper & Row.

MURPHY, JEFFRIE
1973   The Killing of the Innocent. *The Monist*, 54: 527–50.
1976   Rationality and the Fear of Death. *The Monist*, 59: 187–203.

NAGEL, THOMAS
1970   Death, *Noûs*, IV: 73–80. Reprinted in James Rachels (ed.), *Moral Problems*, New York: Harper & Row.

NATANSON, MAURICE
1968   Humanism and Death. In Paul Kurtz (ed.), *Moral Problems in Contemporary Society*, Englewood Cliffs, N.J.: Prentice-Hall.

NATHANSON, JEROME
1969   The Right to Die. *The Ethical Platform*. New York: The New York Society for Ethical Culture, March 2.

NELL, ONORA
1975   Lifeboat Earth. *Philosophy and Public Affairs*, 4: 273–92.

NEGOVSKII, V. A.
1962   *Resuscitation and Artificial Hypothermia* (trans. B. Haigh). New York: Consultants Bureau.

NOTE
1952   The Failure to Rescue: A Comparative Survey. *Columbia Law Review*, 52: 631–47.

PARKINSON, DWIGHT
1973   Criteria for Death. *Journal of Neurosurgery*, 38: 399.

PENELHUM, TERENCE
1970   *Survival and Disembodied Existence*. London: Routledge and Kegan Paul.

PENIN, H., and KÄUFER, C.
1969   *Der Hirntod*. Stuttgart: Georg Thieme Verlag.
1973   Kriterien des Zerebralen Todes aus Neurologischer Sicht. In Krösl and Scherzer (1973, pp. 19–26).

PHILLIPS, D. Z.
1970   *Death and Immortality*. London and Basingstoke: Macmillan.

PLANTINGA, ALVIN
1974   *The Nature of Necessity*. Oxford: Oxford University Press.

PLATO
1961   *The Collected Dialogues of Plato*. Ed. Edith Hamilton and Huntingdon Cairns, New York: Bollingen Foundation.

POLLOCK, JOHN L.
1976   *Subjunctive Reasoning*. Dordrecht: Reidel.

PONTOPPIDAN, HENNING

1976   Optimum Care for Hopelessly Ill Patients, A Report of the Clinical Care Committee of the Massachusetts General Hospital. *New England Journal of Medicine*, 295: 362–64.

PÖRN, INGMAR

1971   *The Logic of Power*. Oxford: Blackwell.
1974   Some Basic Concepts of Action. *Logical Theory and Semantics*. In Soren Stenlund (ed.), Dordrecht: Reidel, pp. 93–101.

PRICE, H. H.

1972   *Essays in the Philosophy of Religion*. London: Oxford University Press.

PRIOR, ARTHUR

1967   *Past, Present and Future*. Oxford: Oxford University Press.

PUCCETTI, ROLAND

1976   The Conquest of Death. *The Monist*, 59: 249–63.

PURTILL, RICHARD

1973   Disembodied Survival. *Sophia*, XII: 1–10.

QUINLAN CASE

1975   *In re* Karen Quinlan: An Alleged Incompetent. Superior Court of New Jersey, Chancery Division, Morris County, Docket No. C-201-75.

RABKIN, MITCHELL T.

1976   Orders Not to Resuscitate. *New England Journal of Medicine*, 295: 364–66.

RACHELS, JAMES

1971   *Moral Problems*. New York: Harper & Row.
1975   Active and Passive Euthanasia. *New England Journal of Medicine*, 292: 78–80.

RAMSAY, PAUL

1970   *The Patient as Person*. New Haven: Yale University Press.

RATCLIFFE, JAMES M.

1966   *The Good Samaritan and the Law*. Garden City, N.Y.: Doubleday.

RAY, J. J., and NAJMAN, J.

1974   Death Anxiety and Death Acceptance: A Preliminary Approach. *Omega*, 5: 311–15.

RESCHER, NICHOLAS

1969   The Concept of Control. In *Essays in Philosophical Analysis*, ed. Nicholas Rescher. Pittsburgh: University of Pittsburgh Press, pp. 327–53.
1969a The Allocation of Exotic Medical Lifesaving Therapy. *Ethics*, 79: 173–86.
1970   *Scientific Explanation*. New York: The Free Press.
1973   The Ontology of the Possible. In *Logic and Ontology*, ed. Milton K. Munitz. New York: New York University Press.

RICHARDSON, SIR JOHN, ROSENHEIM, SIR MAX, et al.
1970   Report of the Special Committee on Organ Transplantation, *British Medical Journal*, March 21; pp. 750–51.

ROBINSON, R.G.
1972   The Moment of Death. *New Zealand Medical Journal*, editorial, 75: 97–98.
1975   The Recognition of Brain Death. *New Zealand Medical Journal*, editorial, 82: 349.

ROZOVSKY, LORNE E.
1972   The Moment of Death. *Canadian Hospital*, 49: 24–25.

RUDIKOFF, SONYA
1974   The Problem of Euthanasia. *Commentary*, 57: 62–68.

RUSSELL, O. RUTH
1974   Moral and Legal Aspects of Euthanasia. *The Humanist*, 34: 22–27.
1975   *Freedom to Die*. New York: Human Sciences Press.

RYLE, GILBERT
1973   Negative Actions. *Hermathena*, Summer: 81–93.

SANFORD, DAVID H.
1976   Killing and Letting Die. Unpublished paper. Abstract in Program Bulletin of the 74th Annual Meeting of the American Philosophical Association, pp. 34–35.

SCHEFFLER, ISRAEL
1963   *The Anatomy of Inquiry*. New York: Knopf.

SCIENTIFIC AMERICAN BOOK
1973   *Life and Death in Medicine*. San Francisco: W. H. Freeman and Co.

SHAW, ANTHONY
1973   The Dilemmas of "Informed Consent" in Children. *New England Journal of Medicine*, 289: 885–90.

SHERWIN, BYRON L.
1974   Jewish Views on Euthanasia. *The Humanist*, 34: 19–21.

SHIBLES, WARREN
1974   *Death: An Interdisciplinary Analysis*. Wisconsin: The Language Press.

SHNEIDMAN, EDWIN, FARBEROW, NORMAN, and LITMAN, ROBERT
1970   *The Psychology of Suicide*. New York: Science House.

SHUSTERMAN, LISA ROSEMAN
1973   Dying and Death: A Critical Review of the Literature. *Nursing Outlook*, 21: 465–71.

SIDEL, V. W.
1972   Resuscitation: Who Makes the Decision?, *The New Physician*, 21: 589–611.

SIEGLER, FREDERICK
1968   Omissions. *Analysis*, 28: 99–106.

SKEGG, P. D. G.
1974   Irreversibly Comatose Individuals: "Alive" or "Dead"? *Cambridge Law Journal*, 33: 130–44.

SKILLMAN, J.
1974   Ethical Dilemmas in the Care of the Critically Ill. *Lancet*, 7881: 634–37.

SLATER, ELIOT
1970   Death: The Biological Aspect. In Downing (1970), pp. 49–60.

SLOTE, MICHAEL A.
1975   Existentialism and the Fear of Dying. *American Philosophical Quarterly*, 12: 17–28.

SMITH, D. H.
1974   On Letting Some Babies Die. *Hastings Center Studies*, 2: 37–46.

SNYDER, O. C.
1949   Liability for Negative Conduct. *Virginia Law Review*, 35: 446–80.

ST. JOHN-STEVAS, N.
1961   *Life, Death, and the Law*. Bloomington: Indiana University Press.

STALNAKER, ROBERT
1968   A Theory of Conditionals. In *Studies in Logical Theory*, ed. Nicholas Rescher. Blackwell: Oxford.

STEINFELS, PETER, and VEATCH, ROBERT
1975   *Death Inside Out: The Hastings Center Report*. New York: Harper & Row.

SULLIVAN, MICHAEL T.
1973   The Dying Person—His Plight and His Right. *New England Law Review*, 8: 197–216.

SUMNER, L. W.
1976   A Matter of Life and Death. *Noûs*, 10: 145–71.

SUPPES, PATRICK
1970   *A Probabilistic Theory of Causality*. Amsterdam: North-Holland.

SUSSER, MERVYN
1973   *Causal Thinking in the Health Sciences*. London: Oxford University Press.

SWIFT, JONATHAN
1961   *Gulliver's Travels*. New York: Norton.

TAYLOR, LOREN F.
1971   A Statutory Definition of Death in Kansas. *Journal of the American Medical Association*, 215: 296.

TEMPLER, D. I.
1970   The Construction and Validation of a Death Anxiety Scale. *The Journal of General Psychology*, 82: 165–77.

THOMAS, LOUIS-VINCENT
1975   Mort et Langage en Occident. *Archives de Sciences Sociales des Religions*, 39: 45–60.

THOMASON, RICHMOND, H.
1970   Indeterminist Time and Truth-value Gaps. *Theoria*, 3: 264–81.

THOMSON, JUDITH JARVIS
1971   The Time of a Killing. *Journal of Philosophy*, LXVIII: 115–32.
1973   Rights and Deaths. *Philosophy and Public Affairs*, 2: 146–59.
1975   Killing, Letting Die, and the Trolley Problem. *The Monist*, 59: 204–17.

TORREY, E.
1968   *Ethical Issues in Medicine*. Boston: Little, Brown & Co.

TOOLEY, MICHAEL
1972   Abortion and Infanticide. *Philosophy and Public Affairs*, 2: 37–65.
1976   *The Termination of Life*: *Some Issues*. Xeroxed manuscript. Research School of Social Sciences, The Australian National University.
1976a Critical Notice of Kluge (1975). *Canadian Journal of Philosophy*, VI: 339–57.

TOYNBEE, ARNOLD
1968   *Man's Concern with Death*. London: Hodder and Stoughton.

TRAMMELL, RICHARD L.
1975   Saving and Taking Life. *Journal of Philosophy*, 72: 131–37.
1976   Tooley's Moral Symmetry Principle. *Philosophy and Public Affairs*, 5: 305–13.

VAN EVRA, JAMES
1971   On Death as a Limit. *Analysis*, 31: 170–77.

VAN TILL-D'AULNIS DE BOUROUILL, ADRIENNE
1971   Medicolegal Aspects of the End of Human Life. Excerpta Medica 59A. *Neurology and Neurosurgery*, 24: 991–92.
1975   How Dead Can You Be? *Medicine, Science and the Law*, 15: 133–47.
1976   Diagnosis of Death in Comatose Patients under Resuscitation Treatment: A Critical Review of the Harvard Report. *American Journal of Law and Medicine*, 2: 1–40.
1976a Legal Aspects of the Definition and Diagnosis of Death. In *Handbook of Clinical Neurology*, ed. P. J. Vinken and G. W. Bruyn, vol 24, part II. Amsterdam and Oxford: North-Holland, pp. 787–828.

VAUX, KENNETH
1974   *Biomedical Ethics*: *Morality for the New Medicine*. New York: Harper & Row.

VEATCH, ROBERT M.
1972   Brain Death. *Hastings Center Report*, II: 10–13.
1972a   Choosing Not to Prolong Dying. *Medical Dimensions*, December, pp. 8–10.
1975   The Whole-Brain Oriented Concept of Death: An Outmoded Philosophical Formulation. *Journal of Thanatology*, 3: 13–30.

VICKERY, K. O.
1974   Euthanasia. *Royal Society of Health Journal*, 94: 118–22.

VOLTAIRE, JEAN FRANCOIS MARIE AROUET DE
1937   *Candide and Other Tales*. London: Dent.

VOLUNTARY EUTHANASIA BILL
1969   *Parliamentary Debates on Voluntary Euthanasia Bill*. House of Lords Official Report, vol. 300, no. 50, March 25.

VON WRIGHT, G. H.
1968   *An Essay in Deontic Logic and the General Theory of Action*. Amsterdam: North-Holland.

VOVELLE, MICHEL
1975   Les Attitudes devant La Mort, Front Actual de l'Histoire des Mentalities. *Archives de Sciences Sociales des Religions*, 39: 17–30.

WAISMANN, FRIEDRICH
1965   *The Principles of Linguistic Philosophy* (ed. R. Harre). London: Macmillan.

WALKER, A. EARL
1974   The Death of a Brain. *Johns Hopkins Medical Journal*, 124: 190–201.

WALTERS, LEROY
1975   *Bibliography of Bioethics*, vol. I. Detroit: Gale Research Co.

WALTON, DOUGLAS N.
1974   Control. *Behaviorism*, 2: 162–71.
1975   Modal Logic and Agency. *Logique et Analyse*, 69–70: 103–111.
1976a   Time and Modality in the *Can* of Opportunity. In *Action Theory*, ed. Myles Brand and Douglas Walton. Dordrecht: Reidel, pp. 271–87.
1976b   Logical Form and Agency. *Philosophical Studies*, 29: 75–89.
1976c   Active and Passive Euthanasia. *Ethics*, 86: 269–74.
1976d   The Logic of Ability. *Philosophy Research Archives*, II: 1.
1976e   On the Rationality of Fear of Death. *Omega*, 7: 1–10.
1977   Critical Study of Some Recent Action Theory. *Philosophia*, in press.

WECHT, C. H.
1969   Determination of Death. *Bulletin of the Allegheny College Medical Society*, 58: 29–34.

WEISMAN, AVERY D., and KASTENBAUM, ROBERT
1968   *The Psychological Autopsy: A Study of the Terminal Phase of Life*. New York: Behavioral Publications, Inc.

WEISMAN, AVERY D.
1972   *On Dying and Denying*: *A Psychiatric Study of Terminality*. New York: Behavioral Publications, Inc.
1974   *The Realization of Death*. New York and London: Jason Aronson.

WERTENBAKER, LAEL TUCKER
1957   *Death of a Man*. New York: Bantam Books.

WHITE, R. J., WOLIN, L. R., MASSOPUT, L. C., TASLITZ, N., and VERDURA, J.
1971   Primate Cephalic Transplantation: Neurogenic Separation, Vascular Association. *Transplantation Proceedings*, 3: 602–4.

WILLIAMS, GLANVILLE
1957   *The Sanctity of Life and the Criminal Law*. New York: Alfred Knopf.

WILLIAMS, H. H.
1972   *True Resurrection*. London: Mitchell Beazley.

WITTGENSTEIN, LUDWIG
1961   *Tractatus Logico-Philosophicus*. London: Routledge and Kegan Paul.

WOODS, JOHN
1976   Can Death Be Understood? In *Values and the Quality of Life*, ed. John King-Farlow and William R. Shea. New York: Neale Watson Publications Inc.
1978   *Engineered Death*. Ottawa: University of Ottawa Press, forthcoming.

WYSCHOGROD, EDITH
1973   *The Phenomenon of Death*. New York: Harper & Row.

YOUNG, ROBERT
1970   The Resurrection of the Body. *Sophia*, 9: 1–15.
1976   Voluntary and Nonvoluntary Euthanasia. *The Monist*, 59: 264–83.

Index